"Poetry is important, the poet is not"
— Octavio Paz —

NUMBER EIGHT
2019

EDITOR-IN-CHIEF
RD ARMSTRONG

ART DIRECTOR
CHRIS YESETA

PUBLISHED BY
LUMMOX PRESS

P.O. BOX 5301
SAN PEDRO, CA 90733-5301
WWW.LUMMOXPRESS.COM/LC/

LUMMOX NUMBER EIGHT

©2019 LUMMOX Press

ISBN 978-0-9997784-4-9

First edition

PO Box 5301

San Pedro, CA 90733

www.lummoxpress.com/lc/

Printed in the United States of America

Acknowledgements

Some of these poems have been previously published; all credits are cited at the end of each poem or poems. The Editor-in-Chief gratefully acknowledges the wisdom of all the previous editors who saw the value in these poems.

LUMMOX

Number Eight / 2019

COVER ART: Photo by RD Armstrong

CONTRIBUTING ARTISTS/PHOTOGRAPHERS:

Jay Blommer	Clarinda Harris
Peter Bruun	Jackie Joice
Chuka Chesney	Norman Olson
Kit Courter	Raindog
Beverly Collins	Jen Dunford-Roskos
Steve Dalachinsky	T. K. Splake
Theresa Dvoracek	Patti Sullivan
Alexis Fancher	Unknown photographer
Dennis Formento	Richard Vidan
Charles Harmon	

TABLE OF CONTENTS

TABLE OF CONTENTS

ANGELA CONSOLO MANKIEWICZ POETRY PRIZE
THIS YEAR'S JUDGE: ELLARAINE LOCKIE

WINNERS

POETRY II

TABLE OF CONTENTS

Frank D. supports L8 - Theresa Dvoracek

TABLE OF CONTENTS

MICRO FICTION

ARTICLES

REVIEWS

CONTRIBUTORS

THE VIEW FROM DOWN HERE

by RD Armstrong

FIRST THINGS FIRST

THIS YEAR more than ever, I am indebted to the PATRONS without whom I don't know where I would be (not that I'm saying that I'd be out on the street but I'd certainly be living on Top Ramen – definitely off my diet). To that end, a big heartfelt thanks to the following (listed in order of their donations): *Georgia Cox, Thomas Brod, Kit Courter, Rolland Vasin, Bill Gainer, H. Lamar Thomas, Michael Meloan, Tony Moffeit, John Donahoe, Alexis Fancher, Mark Evans, Debbi Brody.*

And while we're on the subject, a big "Hell Yeah!" goes out to the intrepid *Yazoota* who, even though he retired last year after 21 years of service to LUMMOX, decided that he'd continue to work on this anthology; as this project is as much his baby as it is mine!

I'm almost through doling out 'gratefuls'.... *Kit Courter* volunteered to go with me on my annual sojourn to Santa Fe, New Mexico in late June and I can't stop gushing about what a great traveling companion he was! I had no idea that going away could be so calming (I always travel alone)....I

Kit Courter Reading –
Photo by Raindog

actually enjoyed myself (even felt content for a couple of days, but don't spread it around, I have a reputation to maintain). Since New Mexico has been brought up, let me tell you a little about this 2300 mile trip....

AROUND THE WAY

(Caution, I must warn you that this will be a bumpy ride)

Each year, since 2013, I have been making a trip out to this beautiful state. Before that, I went out there sporadically (spanning back into the 80's). Since 2013 I've been going to Santa Fe to conduct group readings for the LUMMOX Poetry Anthology. Generally speaking, the LUMMOX contingent from Santa Fe has enjoyed my company and my silly repartee as MC for many summers. But lately, the driving has taken a toll on me as I fade into geezerhood. So, I decided to ask someone to go with me on this trip and I got very lucky with Kit. He drove about 60% of the time, was a fount of information about the geography that zipped by, split the gas and food with me, and let me sleep on the bed while he slept on the living room floor! In addition to all that, he represented the South Bay with his unpretentious, sincere readings at both of the group reads that I put together (the group readings -2- were for last year's LUMMOX Anthology #7).

There are usually at least 20 poets from the Santa Fe area in each issue of the LUMMOX, so the readings can be fun, if not interesting. But I hadn't realized that I'd fallen into a rut over the past 3 or 4 years. I'd taken the fun out of going out there and turned it into something I had to do. It happened so slowly, I hadn't really noticed it. But it was this trip that I realized what the difference was. It was the 'burden of the schedule'. In the past, I had a schedule to keep and if it wasn't on the schedule, well I just couldn't do it. There was a schedule (1) for sleeping arrangements (one night here, two nights there), (2)visiting (I love to chat and most of the people I know out there are awfully interesting), (3) eating, (4) pushing the books that I had brought out that trip (selling the books without

looking too pathetic – because the whole point of the trip is to sell enough to offset the costs of gas, and food) and of course, (5) managing the reading(s) promotion and making sure that I brought the LUMMOX "Pop-up Store" (books, Tee Shirts, Mugs, Book Bags)... Oh yeah, almost forgot, (6) recording the events (photos and video)!

(Side note): The natural wear and tear on a 68 year old body is exacerbated by my Diabetes and the myriad of things that can go wrong, including the tendency of superficial wounds (like blisters) turning into life-threatening amputation sites! This is another source of worry and fear.

So, you see that I have a lot of stuff to worry about. Managing 6 schedules is stressful enough, as well as getting out there and back on Route 40. I've driven a lot across the western United States (maybe 100,000 miles). All this alone. A couple of times I thought I'd go mad just watching miles of desert rolling by. Only two times have I had a companion on a trip, once in 2011, with G. Murray Thomas (we took an epic road trip up into and across Colorado, dropping down into New Mexico and then heading back to L.A. via Flagstaff, Arizona). It was at least 3000 miles long. And 8 years later, I took this trip with Kit Courter (a mere 2300 miles).

I think moving around from night to night generates more stress than I can deal with comfortably (tho I used to be able to handle it fine, 6 years ago). This year, instead of having multiple lodgings, I made an arrangement for us to stay at a quaint little 3 room 'shack' about 10 miles southwest of Santa Fe. It's known as the Pump House and it belongs to Argos Mac-Callum, owner and operator of Teatro Paraguas (site of one of our readings) in Santa Fe. He's been living on this piece of property for something like 60 years, can you imagine? I'm excited to have lived here in Long Beach for 21. But 60?! Whoa Nelly!

The Pump House (it also houses the well head) has finished walls and ceilings, windows and doors and it's so far off the beaten path that we never locked the door. It has electricity and a privy (outhouse) about 50 feet away....but there were a few things that would have made it more bearable. *One*, there was no indoor plumbing, no running water; so no showers/baths (tho there was a nice big tub near the privy which I suppose would be a comfort on those hot summer days). Kit said it was like camping / backpacking. Besides we were guys...this was definitely not for the ladies (unless they were adventurous). We were two, happy, old men, living rough and enjoying the solace of the desert. We were so innocent, it was making me kinda weird!

The *second thing* was a blackout that made contact with the outside world nearly impossible... no cell service and no wifi, so we had to go into town to take care of "Admin". This is where Starbucks came in handy. But we'd get breakfast first, then hit Starbucks, then poke around a bit and before heading to one of the two readings, or back to our 'rancherito', or stopping first at Trader Joe's to buy some salads and cold meats and something to drink (I was accosted one time by a guy spouting something that sounded vaguely familiar....turned out to be Yeats. I guess he was responding to one of my LUMMOX shirts. I was kinda scared by his intensity, as he followed me thru the aisles demonstrating his 'mad' poetry skills. Eventually, he gave up). We also found some premium herb, making for some interesting conversations and jam sessions. This is where I realized that I had forgotten most of the songs I knew! Thankfully, I soon forgot how bummed I was (I was distracted by something)...because I have the *Short Term Memory Loss*, which is a blessing and a curse. I now wrangle with remembering simple tasks like taking my meds or eating at a regular time or getting to bed at a decent hour. All this would depress me because it is seemingly out of my control, but thanks to Zoloft, I hardly ever get depressed and if I do it doesn't last more than a few hours (much better than the 6 months it used to last).

Speaking of Zoloft, I've been having fragmented memories of my old man, back when I was a lad. Might be because of the big earthquake on the 5th of July that we had. When I came out here with my ma and pa -- we were *new* in Ridgecrest, California (earthquake) – they were newly married, I was *new* by about 6 months, pa got a job at China Lake Naval Test Facility (epicenter) and our lives were moving along. I miss that. Being part of a family; tho some would say that I have an extended family through the books I have published and all the poets I know. But really these poets are just acquaintances, I've never met most of them. I do have about fifteen hundred *friends* on FaceBook, but I don't really *know* them. The ones I do know are the ones that I meet along the way, at readings or in my daily wanderings. Even though I treat them like a friend, they don't always respond like one, which is very disappointing.

I've been accused of not respecting Canadian poets, (also accused of committing fraud!) and this after I had published the anthology called **Tamaracks**, which is a survey of Canadian Poetry from one hundred and thirteen of Canada's elder poets (mostly). I could have sworn off all Canadian Poetry after dealing with the editor's unprofessionalism. We had a falling out (to put it mildly). But I'm happy to report that about fourteen Canadians applied and eleven were accepted for this issue.

It was just about this time last year, late June I think, that the editor and I got into it (tho, really, we didn't get into it because he *refused* to respond to all communication, for *two months*). I was already fighting a deadline for last year's LUMMOX and I should have dropped the Canadian Project and eaten the $900 I had already invested in it (but my budget is so tight, there's no way I could realistically do that), so I forged onward. In the end, it was a gigantic clusterfuck. I grimace whenever I think about it.

I did learn a few things: *as dementia drags me deeper into the rabbit hole, I find I need to ask for help, more and more, and that it's okay to do that! I've gotten pretty good at it over the past decade or so. But, as I get older, I also need to simplify the tasks it takes to bring a book project to fruition. Finally, I have to stop, or at least, lay down the law, before I take on a new project so that everyone starts on the same page.*

3 Room Shack –
Photo by Raindog

NEWS

Some Walt Whitman Bicentennial things to do:

There are still a few things scheduled for the end of the year out east. So, if you're curious about Uncle Walt, here are some options...

August 31 - November 30
Camden County Historical Society
1900 Park Blvd.
Camden, NJ 08103

October 3 - December 14
Center for Book Arts
28 West 27th Street, 3rd Floor
New York, NY 10001

October 15 - January 5, 2020
Providence Athenaeum
https://providenceathenaeum.org/

I hear Camden is lovely this time of year!

PROJECTS PENDING

In other news, I'm getting ready to jump right back into it: two or three books, by other poets, in line for publication, rebuild the LUM-

*Tamaracks reader
Eva Kolacz*

MOX website, fire up the promotional machine and move the LUMMOX Poetry Anthology out of print and on-line. I'm doing this (well, planning for it, at least) because it seems like wherever one loses one's marbles, dementia is nearby. Couple more years, I'll be seventy and if I don't do something soon I'm gonna have to quit and forget I was ever here... and I sure don't want that to happen!

WHAT'S IN THIS ISSUE

POETRY

There is poetry, lots of it, some of the best I've seen in awhile. There are the three winners of the **Angela Consolo Mankiewicz Poetry Prize** (named after the poet, essayist, reviewer, composer and friend, who passed away from non-smokers lung cancer in early 2017). They are: *Nancy Shiffrin*, first place, and *Austin Alexis*, second place and *B.J. Buckley*, third place. Nancy lives in Santa Monica, CA and I've known her for a long time and published her in various anthologies (including this one). Austin is from New York City and even tho I don't know him, he has an impressive bio (I'd be curious to know how he found his way here). B.J. Lives in Power, MT. I had the opportunity to publish her book, **Corvidae**, a few years back. It had 4 beautiful woodblock prints. BTW Corvidae refers to the crow family (ravens, black birds, crows and more).

The contest was judged by *Ellaraine Lockie*, a poet I've known for at least twenty years and one who has become a part of the LUMMOX family (she has always shown me kindness and friendship). She is widely published and awarded as a poet, nonfiction book author and essayist. **Tripping with the Top Down** is her thirteenth chapbook. Earlier collections have won Poetry Forum's Chapbook Contest Prize, San Gabriel Valley Poetry Festival Chapbook Competition, Encircle Publications Chapbook Contest, Best Individual Poetry Collection Award from *Purple Patch* magazine in England, and *the Aurorean's* Chapbook Choice Award. Ellaraine teaches writing workshops and serves as Poetry Editor for the lifestyles magazine, *Lilipoh*.

MICRO-FICTION

Then in the Micro-fiction section, there are a variety of little stories by some writers who range from bent to warped in their fiction mindset. They are RD Armstrong – **Fear Moves to a New Town** (from his Manx Tales series); Seven Dhar – **The Shaman**; Helen Donahoe - **Lives Change**; Alexis Fancher - **She Says Stalker / He Says Fan**; Roseanna Frechette – **For Sarah**; Michael Meloan – **Papoulis**; Jeanine Stevens – **The Language of Corn**; H. Lamar Thomas – **A Red Mule Named Red Mule**; and Felice Zoota-Lucero – **You Can Call Me Mom**.

As Tom Waits once said "They all came from good families but somewhere along the line they just got kinda weird!"

ARTICLES / ESSAYS

In June, I was surprised to hear that this is the bicentennial of Walt Whitman's birth year (a vision just surged through my imagination as a flash mob of academics danced around a giant statue of Uncle Walt while the rest of the poetry rabble get on with their ignorant lives), so I had to throw in my two cents with the article, **Walt Whitman – Radical Optimist?** I asked Gil Hagen Hill to help me out with his poem, **We Was Robbed** and Henry Crawford came in with a nice poem entitled **Walt Whitman Ekphrastic**. Then there's **Poetry X Hunger: Looking into the Empty Cupboard** by Hiram Larew. This is a project that Hiram has been working on for several years with the goal in mind to tackle

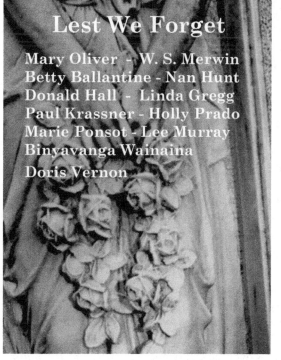

Lest We Forget

Mary Oliver - W. S. Merwin
Betty Ballantine - Nan Hunt
Donald Hall - Linda Gregg
Paul Krassner - Holly Prado
Marie Ponsot - Lee Murray
Binyavanga Wainaina
Doris Vernon

world hunger, no less! A worthy cause, indeed. Then we have an excerpt from **Acetylene Sunsets**, a new book of selected essays (due out this year from LUMMOX Press), **Tony Scibella: the Poet in America** by John Macker. This is a memoir of sorts as Macker knew Tony back in the day. **Homage to Pierre Seghers, French Publisher and Songwriter-Poet (1906-1987)** by Basia Miller is an essay about one of the most influential poets / songwriters of his time. Through his publishing house, he brought French poetry out of the "dark ages" (of lyrical expression) into a more expanded, reality based world view, using all styles including free verse. For thirty years from 1939 to 1969 his influence spread across France, through WWII and subsequent crisises, Pierre was the *Quincey Jones* of French Culture. I think it's a fascinating article and I hope you will agree... Imagine being a hungry fly on the wall of *Allen Ginsburg's* Haight Ashberry address, listening to the intellectual conversations over some delish dish recipes... Can you? By reading this article, **Eating And Drinking With The Beats (part one)** by Charles Plymell, perhaps you'll understand. Plymell was an integral part of the beat experience and still has a hand in the game today. This next rather personal essay came by way of an email exchange. It was sent as a sort of bio by Ms. Ramirez but it was too long for a bio and too short for an essay. I was pleased when she took me up on my request for more details (to be more informational not

Glass Casting – Photo by Raindog

more grisley). The result is **Living on the Edge** by Coco Ramirez. It's an insight into what many of us struggle with, finding and keeping our balance. **Memories of Hubert "Cubby" Selby** by M. G. Stephens is a remembrance of a different time in Brooklyn, NY and a book entitled **Last Exit to Brooklyn**. Perhaps Mr. Plymell knew Hubert Selby too. This guy actually has a lot of friends. **ANTS** by G. Murray Thomas explores the relationship between the group (or 'superorganism') and the individual. He uses ants as an example. I found it interesting, so here it is. Finally, an interesting article on Norman Olson, artist and poet, who's work has been seen by thousands of readers of Small Press magazines and books over the last twenty years or so. **Notes on the Drawings of Norman Olson** by Bill Tremblay provides some insight into Olson's work. He is one of the most prolific artists I know (his work has been featured in most of these LUMMOX issues).

Reviews

The Blues Drink Your Dreams Away – Selected Poems (1983 – 2018) by John Macker
    Reviewed by RD Armstrong.... A rare full length review of John Macker's latest collection. Good stuff (in the book, not so much the review).

Café Crazy by Francine Witte
    Reviewed by Linda Lerner. Linda is no slouch in the poetry dept. herself and if she applauds a book then I can endorse it too. I trust her implicitly.

New Found Land by Carolyn Clark
    Reviewed by Thelma T. Reyna, Ph.D. Dr. Reyna was very impressed by this book! It seems to lay bare with surgical precision the delicate issues that worry us. This from the review "thoughts and values find themselves voiced elegantly in this book, much to the enrichment and contentment of our collective souls!"

Fairfax and Other Poems by David Del Bourgo
    Reviewed by Nancy Shiffrin. While this is an old review, the work of the poet, David Del Bourgo, still holds up according to Ms. Shiffrin. Worth checking out.

Flow by Robin Scofield
    Reviewed by Donna Snyder. *"Robin Scofield's book is well named as both the poet and the poems in it epitomize the diverse theories of flow, a law, not a theory, that can be seen as applying to everything from the design of leaves to the natural pattern of rivers. Its organizational principles are found in fractals and snowflakes, as well as the writing and performance of poetry. Flow is an excellent book and I recommend it to anyone who is interested in the topography of the Southwestern United States or the application of scientific theory in the writing of poetry."* (Excerpted from Donna's review)

LET'S GET TO THE POETRY...

POETRY I

Alexis Fancher - Dusk in L.A.

The Better Mousetrap - Revisited

A friend of mine
was explaining
why I shouldn't
get the new, more
"humane" mousetraps
but should stick to
the tried and true
steel spring models.
Apparently the new
traps just glue the
mice in place
inside a little card
board coffin – which
makes it easier to
dispose of their little
mouse carcasses. So
instead of breaking
their little necks/or backs
with a "snap trap"
they just panic and end
up chewing their little
legs off and dying a
long drawn-out terrifying
death. And this is the
more *HUMANE* trap,
mind you.

Maybe I'm old-fashioned
but whatever happened to
the good old days:

A piece of cheese
a flashlight
a six-pack
and a twelve gauge?

RD Armstrong
Long Beach, CA

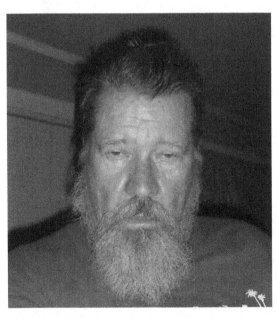

Sad man, tired man - by Raindog

A LIFE GONE

As I think of you-- sadness comes in waves.
Though life for us goes on,
past trauma lingers
Why does healing and forgiveness take
So *long*?

The hearts of offspring not recovered.
The minds and souls of children
So *hurt*.
Now grandchildren are here who only
Know your name.

Belinda Berry
Long Beach, CA

Redacted Poem

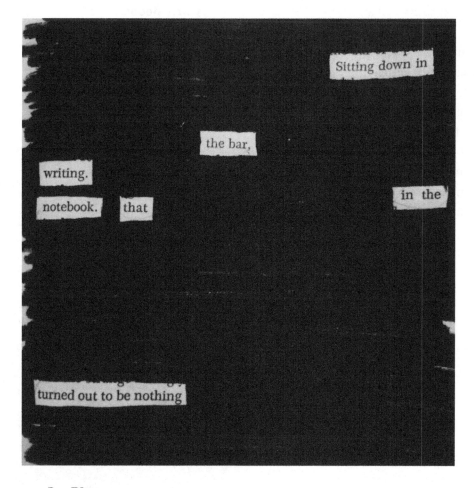

Jay Blommer
Long Beach, CA

File Under "S"

At the Good Friday service
members of the parish
wrote their sins on paper
and one after another
nailed their confessions
to the wooden cross
that was set up near the altar.

After the mass
before I cleaned the carpet
and swept out the narthex
I removed each piece of paper from the cross
and placed them in a ziplock bag.

The anonymous sins
of the congregation
are in storage

in a file cabinet
in my second floor office
near the paint cans
next to the dust mop
and the broken vacuum cleaner.

Chris Bodor
St. Augustine, FL

Kneel, then recline upon my feet
Eve out [...]
Alone on Venice Beach
At night [...]
It is all so slow, so simple
In [...] white [...]
Being a sunset
[...]

COLD ELLISON by PHILOMENE LONG

[...]
Back at the Ellison
[...]
Alone at the black iron gate
[...]
I look up
[...]
Two red brick wings open
[...]
As if to embrace me
[...]
Two ghostly shimmering red wings
[...]
We watch each other
[...] to sleep [...]

THE UNBELIEVABLE TRUTH

A few weeks
before
my father
died of
prostate
cancer
I read him
a new
poem
the phone
went silent
for a long
time
I thought he
must have
fallen
asleep:
"You write
what we feel,
but can't put
into words,"

he said as
I was about
to hang up
I thanked him
and we spoke
for a little longer
about other
things,
I didn't tell him
he was
wrong
that everything
I wanted to
say to him I
couldn't:
not even a
respectable--
goodbye.

Brenton Booth
South Penrith, NSW, Australia

You Get Two Coins

In ancient Greece, when someone died
It was the tradition
To put coins on their eyes.
The heaviness of the coins
Kept the eyelids shut.
There was another reason
For the coins.
The ferryman demanded fare.
The dead could not cross the river Styx
Without the ferry.
But two coins?
How much was the fare?
Was one of those coins
Possibly the fare
For a return trip?
No thanks. I would rather
Not stay here. Take me back.

I can't know what is out there, really.
It might be wonderful.
It might be simply
Another reality on another plane.
But I want to go when I'm ready.
Yet I remember
Times when I was desperate
And was ready to pay that fare.
Sometimes I was quiet about it
And told no one how I felt.
Once or twice I begged for pity
And announced my wish for oblivion
To the dismay of others.
Then I'd say
It was all a joke.
Some joke!
I don't feel it's such a joke
When I hear that now from someone else.

Do I need to feel foolish
Because I grew afraid,
Called around and reached out
As best I could
Only to realize
That someone else
Was desperate and having a joke
And calling for help
In the worst way possible.

Here's a little joke. In my college days,
Studying the Odyssey,
I snuck early into class
And drew a map on the blackboard
Of the Greek afterlife underworld,
The River Styx, with a sign reading
"Good for invulnerability."
My prof was in on that joke and added the words
"Get the heel in."
Who knows what a dunk
In that river
Might do to us
If we aren't planning to swim it
And don't have the fare for the ferry.
Being immune to hurt
Is not what it will do.
Let the transition come when it has to
But not because we want to go.
Message to all who might be thinking
Of swimming that river.
You get two coins.
Two fares.
There is a way back.
Return trip worth taking.

Lynne Bronstein
Van Nuys, CA

The Epitome of Dissonance

What is causing this enormous cacophony
and leaving behind the slivers of isles craving silence?

What is this shrill avalanche that prevents
the heather from enjoying a peaceful nap?

Where does this resounding rasp originate,
leaving behind it a wasteland of sonic dissonance that even a trifle of quietude is unthinkable?

Who roars with such blatant bellicosity
that the water of the isles ripple with such frequency they appear tantamount to boiling?

When will this ferocious sonic turbulence cease
and let an easy breeze caress the bones within the ears of the land and water?

Heath Brougher
York, PA

Raindog

IN THE TEMPLE

Naked
I pray in the temple .
Primal power
Flows like bubbling waters
Up from the boundless reservoir
Deep in the heart of me.
Deep, deep down
 I have ventured
Into the land of the tigers.
Snarling, they lie down,
Tamed by ecstasy.
The lush jungle
Full of fruit
Bursts forth
From the seed.
The root of my being
Searches downward,
Where up and down
Join
In a joy of self revelation.
Rapture reveals
The source of my love
In splendor
I have been reborn,
Touched by the grace of goodness,
Moved
By the measureless heart of love.
It smiles at me
With no equivocation,
An invocation
Evoking
The vast need of the created
Calling, longing to be born.

Dr. Patricia Brown
Santa Fe, NM

Streetlights

We used to stand in front
of the library
on Friday and Saturday nights
wearing our football jackets
red & white
lightning bolts down the sleeves
like stripes;
we said "I shit you not"
and hocked gobs
of pearly spit
onto the sidewalk;
we said—whenever asked if
we had a date—
"my name is in the phone book."
We watched cars go past,
some with a guy and
a girl inside,
and we imagined where
they were going
but not why
and we spat
and watched the streetlights come on,

watched the stars come out;
we said, "let's do something!"
We said, "like what?"
We never went into the library
except to take a piss
or else
follow some girl inside.

Wayne F. Burke
Barre, VT

Published in Chiron Review

Window light - Raindog

Piccoli Pezzi

he closed the door
and entered his world;
he closed his world
and entered his soul

Helmut C. Calabrese
Toms River, NJ

AFTER THE RAIN

Breathe in crisp blue sky from billowy white clouds
floating west to east with San Gabriel mountains
to soprano sax meditation of John Coltrane

Walk to corner of Colorado and Allen to take
Pasadena city bus for breakfast at Corner Bakery
and grocery shop at Trader Joe's located a floor above

After getting off bus change mind to go instead to nearby
Green Street Restaurant where my mother-in-law, Dorothy,
often treated our family to a gourmet breakfast

See they no longer have on menu Otto's Potato Patch omelet
Order instead two scrambled egg-potato tacos
Coffee not hot and ask waitress to bring me one that is

Spot sitting at nearby table spirits of those living
today--Cheryl, Mark and me along with those whose
bodies are no longer with us, Dorothy and Luke

Dorothy, a recently retired nurse, is sitting
between Luke and Mark, her first two grandkids
She worked at the maternity ward where they were born

Cheryl orders eggs benedict, Dorothy, ham and eggs,
Luke and Mark, pancakes covered with strawberries,
and me, Otto's Potato Patch omelet

The eggs benedict looks luscious but Cheryl with soft voice
says eggs are a little bit too hard and asks for new plate
"MOM!" Luke says grinning while rest of us laugh

Clouds flow across cyan skies like flock of swans
above Trader Joe's on corner of Lake and Del Mar
Exhale

A Love Supreme
A Love Supreme
A Love Supreme

Calokie
Pasadena, CA

Ohtsu

I thought I saw
a pile of penguins
bleeding in snow
but no
it was a camellia
flower pouring red
petals on a blanket
its yellow pistol
a dying sun
on a crimson ground
surrounded by flakes
piling up over rocks
and an empty picnic table
where have the people
gone?
they are sensible
not attracted to cold
death by freezing
this disexistence
does not appeal to them
so they are safe
somewhere else
looking out windows
at the white world
slowly burying color
until spring brings
back the recreation
of happy faces
jumping over stones
rolling on grass
plucking flowers from trees
to give to loved ones
while we're breathing
and sweating in the
warmth of it all
seasonally removed
from the danger
of ice falling from
the heavens, oh god
what have we done
to deserve these changes?
that's just the order
of the great
cycle that generates
new life to replace
old weather-beaten
stems of history
turn them into mulch
for babies who grow
into food for predators
who do not go through
unscathed thanks
to the humans capable
of destroying
any creation

Don Kingfisher Campbell
Alhambra, CA

Mulholland Drive

"The car crash on the avenue that leaves blood and memories
scattered in the grass."
Charles Bukowski

The end is the beginning,
there is no changing that now.
All the movies we were cast in
are over, long gone from theaters,
moved to second billing drive ins,
are features the only lovers
left alive, pay no attention to.
Our bodies belong to someone else
now, even as nearly used up as they
are, torn from scripts that should have
had happy endings but never did.
Search and rescue teams find our
remains, once the last vestiges of
life have been squeezed out.
Repurpose them as test crash dummies
up against a laboratory wall.
The scarring that results, makes
what we were, what we imagined
we could be, unrecognizable now.
Even our fingerprints and dental
records reveal nothing.
If life was a comedy ours was not
a funny one.
The once lit candle representing
the souls we have lost, is blown out now.
A night owl watches over us but
there is nothing left to see.

Alan Catlin
Schenectady, NY

Party House

There's a concert going on
across the canyon
one house becomes a nightclub
for private parties
usually we call the non-emergency number
but tonight the operator isn't answering
I could either pull my hair out
or batten down the windows
but it's hot
we need a breeze

Boho Girl - by Chuka Chesney

plus who can drift away
to the wistful erection in his baritone
The singer is wearing anaconda paes
like a spillway of cologne
continuously wheedling
trying to seduce
with a high pitched key
like the riff of coyotes
doesn't make me want to gronts
His unctuous voice hissove
makes me burrow in my pillow
It's quiet for a minute
but my eardrums still pulse
I hear the gusto of the crowd
limos licking the curb
a vibration thrums
the once obsidian night
lit like a chandelier
with amps of decibels
There's the microphone again
polluting our ears
This doesn't feel suburban
It's nouveau riche noise

Chuka Chesney
Glendale, CA

Happiness

You say happiness comes from deep within.

Look inside you--there is potential.

Ignite it and watch it burst into a million colors.

You can do it. You have the tools.

I melt into a river of tears, silently disagreeing
with everything you say.

There is no flame in me, no diamond in my core.

I am Asian, you see.

I have a degree, not inherent self-worth.

It doesn't fill the void, doesn't wipe away the shame.

So take my A's and give me your C's.

I'd rather be you than me.

I'd rather not feel the way I do--
so small that I'm unworthy of a single glance.

Jackie Chou
Pico Rivera, CA

I Am Unhappy

I am unhappy because I like being unhappy.
I am unhappy because I don't like being unhappy.

I am unhappy because people want me to be happy.
I am unhappy because people don't want me to be happy.

I am unhappy because I want to love.
I am unhappy because I don't want to love.

I am unhappy because she loves me.
I am unhappy because she does not love me.

I am unhappy because I love her.
I am unhappy because I don't love her.

I am unhappy because I know how to show her I love her.
I am unhappy because I don't know how to show her I love her.

I am unhappy because I want to leave her.
I am unhappy because I don't want to leave her.

I am unhappy because I want her to leave me.
I am unhappy because I don't want her to leave me.

I am unhappy because I don't want to hurt her.
I am unhappy because I don't want her to hurt me.

I am unhappy because I see the way forward.
I am unhappy because I don't see the way forward.

I am unhappy because I see the way forward and I want to go.
I am unhappy because I see the way forward and I don't want to go.

I am unhappy because I don't see the way forward but I want to see the way forward.
I am unhappy because I don't see the way forward and I don't want to see the way forward.

I am unhappy because I always know what to do.
I am unhappy because I never know what to do.

I am unhappy because I know what to do and want to do it.
I am unhappy because I know what to do and don't want to do it.

I am unhappy because I want to be told what to do.
I am unhappy because I don't want to be told what to do.

I am unhappy because I am writing this poem.
I am unhappy because I am not writing another poem.

Jonathon Church
Alexandria, VA

like dogs

I've tried a few times
to wean off the
get-a-grip pills

thinking I'd like
to be me again
feel feelings without
a filter

but when I try
I can feel I am still
the designated doormat

all those many
boots and heels and
sensible skechers
grinding grit

kicking backwards
like dogs dispersing crap
before trotting off

Wanda Morrow Clevenger
Hettick, IL

Artificial Intelli-gents - Steve Dalachinsky

Two by Sharyl Collin

With Abandon

It was after the howling.
They'd pulled apart, the male
panting in thatched shadows under the elm,
while the female rolled on her back,
stirring up a cloud of dust
before licking herself clean.

My mother sat across the table,
watching the dogs as she tapped
cylinders of ash into a Pepsi can.
Her gaze lifted and my cheeks burned
with something I didn't understand.
I wanted to leave but was afraid
movement would encourage her words.

Her eyes fixed on me as she took a drag
from her cigarette and held it, her words
moving through the smoke.
"Pups'll be along in about 8 weeks."
She nodded toward the yard. "That's the way
all living things get their start."

Her hand moved to the can,
stabbing down the butt until smoke
curled around her fingers, then stopped.
"Even people," she added, turning her eyes
back to the yard, while I tried to imagine
the man who could make her roll
on her back in the dirt.

> **Sharyl Collin**
> Lomita, CA

Walking Stick

Thin limbs
bound by joints that flare
like spider's legs,
my father is becoming one
with his walking stick.

I wonder about the man
who fashioned his stick,
why he chose the crooked branch
to sand and polish,
shoe with rubber tip
and dress in golden handle,

as I wonder
about the grandmother
I never knew, how she felt
when death laid claim
on her left breast

before her son
had finished growing
still needing
to be guided and groomed,

when she so wanted
to be there
to watch him
bloom.

> **Sharyl Collin**
> Lomita, CA

Skyline - by Beverly Collins

See

I see the Sun…hear
laughter at the breakfast table
drinks in hand ready to toast in
the new day.

I see challenge's silhouette outside a
door curtain. Its spindly hand rattles hard
the crystal door knob.

I see the scowl on worry's brow as it enters
the room and carries a belief we are short on
everything except anguish. It has no yeast
to raise any cake.

Again, I see hope mop the area like a free
maid in a delivery room. Hope knows possibility
is coming. It's wet, butt-naked and screaming.

Beverly M. Collins
Burbank, CA

Esperanza

after Ferlinghetti

I have been waiting my whole life to write this poem.

I am waiting to realize my dreams, or, rather, the opportunity to act on them.

I am waiting for a time when love is the purpose of the rule of law.

I am waiting for an era where long lineups, aggressive drivers, and people who won't move back on the bus
    are the biggest problems.

I am waiting for a world where all the –isms disappear, only to be replaced by
tolerance, peace and harmony.

I am waiting for more tolerance, peace and harmony in my own life.

But I know the waiting is good, because it helps me focus and work on what I'm waiting for.

I am waiting to forgive all the people who have wronged me over the years, and myself for all the times I've done wrong.

I am waiting for the end of hangovers…and my reliance on what causes them.

I am waiting to understand the purpose of the chronic pain in my knees, my heart, and my soul.

I am waiting to become patient, and I don't know how much longer I can wait.

I am waiting for her who has waited for me even longer to make our love bloom.

I am waiting for the next coming of my Lord and Saviour, even though He is in my life every day.

I am waiting for other people who call themselves Christians to realize He is coming back to save everyone.

I am waiting for what makes my waiting worthwhile.

Patrick Conners
Toronto, ON CAN.

Esperanza first appeared in the August/September 2016 issue of Canadian Stories magazine. It also featured in Bottom of the Wine Jar, the third instalment of the CCLA Bridging Series, published in January, 2017 by SandCrab Press.

Fall Clean-up

An old man sweeps the flagstone walk to his house,
dispersing Siberian elm leaves, the black ants
living between the stones, torn bits of newspaper.
A raven hunkers down on a branch above him,
offers harsh comments. The man pays no attention
but shuffles back inside the door needing paint,
another hinge pin.

In the next strong gust of wind, leaves from piles
swept to the side twirl and dance across the path.
Already ants return. Indoors, the man takes off
his shoes, rests his feet on a stool and turns on
the television, flips channels often, his wife
no longer there to object, though he wishes
she were raising her voice. TV noise
doesn't mask the silence.

Blair Cooper
Santa Fe, NM

Smiling Totem - Raindog

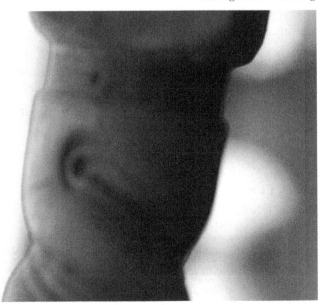

Two by Kit Courter

Libraries of Graves

I followed your passage
through lives turning like seasons through the years,
seeking there your mysteries, things lost, questions un-requited,
wondering how to remember you.

How long does memory last? How many centennials until
stone monuments   melt into grass
as turf covers our molders cast in clay?

I had hoped to feel your presence
and trusted fate to shield me there from malice,
from essences of death,
from things long ago laid low — but I felt
nothing, only wind blowing autumn leaves,
light rain drifting down from a sky glowing gray with cloud,
soft sod beneath my feet.

Your secrets, once chiseled into stone,
are safe from my prying eyes, holding in abeyance
any knowing of your days,
lost in ephemeral libraries of graves.

— Williamsport, Pennsylvania

Kit Courter
Torrance, CA

Desert Mountains - by Kit Courter

Victory Lap

Hey, old friend
why don't we pull up a couple of chairs
out on your front deck
and smoke a little herb —
sit out there like the couple of grey old short-dicked codgers we've become
and shave chips off the universe as does a plane.   We'll pick up

each flake — and give it a smile of recognition
as we find the humor in each of their cut sides —
recognizing their moral lessons and
the silly shortcomings of their actors. You know, I'll bet we'll both
just bust-a-gut over how many times we've backed ourselves
into those same corners,

or strode into what looked like an open door,
or just plain stumbled along with our attention behind our eyes.
You and I, we have seen "The Griz", we have!
— and the fox that plotted itself into our bank accounts,
the god dammed raccoons that raided our pantries.
But, you know — none of that matters anymore!

as we watch a hummingbird testing flowers for nectar
and just enjoy each others company, letting time go by,
spinning remembered stories into artful yarns
during the final years of our turn
at the miracle of life.

Kit Courter
Torrance, CA

To Our Kids

We're senior delinquents
modeling our lives after those times when they were so new
and all the rules were irrelevant disruptions
to everything we felt and experienced.

Our passions weren't lived to their full potential
and now we want to make up for our omissions.
But we can't help but notice you down there,
the same as we were.

Destined be be the same as we are.

To us you are equally amusing
and horrifying.
All the baroque seriousness you place on your little lives.

You have no idea the tangle of trouble ahead of you.
The useless energy you'll spend on desperate
subterfuge and out and out lies.
You have no idea of the nowhere it'll get you in the end.

You have plans. You have dreams.
You have lessons to teach and children to raise to be just like you.

A cookbook life.

But you have no idea what's really going on around you.
There is a complex wind blowing just above your heads.
Maybe if you stood up taller and noticed us
we could avoid all this.

We can't really blame you, though,
what with all the commercial viability you represent
and all the raw material you wield
and all that is at stake.
And all the sales pitches whirling around you.
It's tough. We don't deny that.

None of that means we can't enjoy a bit of fun at your expense.
Laugh a little at your predictable foibles.
God knows we deserve it.
No one takes us seriously anyway.

So, enjoy it all. It's yours. But do try to relax a little now and again.
And remember what we have said.
Because soon we will be gone and you will be us.

William Craychee
Wernersville, PA

LET ME TELL YOU

Let me tell you of my love in sweet tones,
but more is told by my eyes.
My voice is soft and mellow, it drones,
and my demeanor tells you, there are no lies.

Feel the sweetness of how much I care,
nothing is hidden under a false guise.
Just the knowing we have a lifetime to share,

and that you'll always be, for me, that Grand Passion,
the love, the heart beat, that never goes out of fashion.

Sue Crisp
Shingle Springs, CA

Settling the Color Question

The days are gone when Aunt Maggie
and her friend Mary Grace argued
with such vigor whether yellow
or some green was my best color.
"Just look at those green eyes," one says.

"But look at that dark hair against
that soft yellow," the other one notes.
I'd worn my morning yellow sunshine suit
to lunch at Stouffer's with the gals.
Down from Duquesne where my aunt paid
my first semester tuition
ant the American Legion
heard mother's plea for a vet's girl
and the Feds pitched in a nice loan
after I swore my allegiance
and supplemented with two jobs.
"College has changed you,: my aunt notes,
disappointed, though that's the point.
My looks no longer were the point.

Ann Curran
Pittsburgh, PA

Ten Minutes

It's only ten minutes, I know.
And indeed, that's not a whole lot,
But in less time than that, I'll show,
How much for my time, I got.

The ten extra minutes, I did
Hear my alarm and reset it.
While under my pillow I hid,
From getting up, which I dreaded.

With ten extra minutes, on my walk
To the bus stop, where I board,
I heard the robins sing and squawk,
That in haste I often ignored.

At noon time my ten minutes brought
A break in my daily routine,
And a quiet respite is sought,
In the park, enjoying the scene.

And still later on, at twilight,
Curled up in my library's nook,
Was ten minutes more of pure delight,
Engrossed in my favorite book.

Ten minutes is valuable time.
Quite often it's more than we need.
It took ten minutes to pen this rhyme
And less than ten minutes to read.

Helen Donahoe
Pittsburgh, PA

Green

Repeat the word silently, allow the mind crowd
with names, images: Seurat's pointillistic landscapes,
Gauguin's foliage, El Greco's Toledo, Sorolla's sea.

Turn the page, look outside, chlorophyll performs
miracles daily, silvery spears on olive trees,
sharp needles on pines, emeralds on rice fields.

It suggests water, fertility, a fresh presence
enhancing arcaded cloisters, tenderness
in new shoots, young, intrepid, not quite ripe.

Avarice in Shylock's eyes, Cain's envy of Abel,
indescribable fear etched into Perseus's face
terrified of locking eyes with Medusa.

Verdigris over copper ornaments, bronze swords,
mined from the ancient Latin well of viridis,
verdant vigor on my mother's thumb.

At 16 I had a boyfriend, eyes the inside color
of Romaine lettuce, a smile of berries and kisses.
When the sun choked with jealousy collapsed

in the mountain town where weeping willows grow,
hopped to the lake, cool moss clinging to stones,
swam under a moon resolute in turning our skin
green.

Alicia Viguer-Espert
Los Angeles, CA

Published in Spectrum 18

an informal letter of homage
to allen ginsberg—now dead

america
you are an enigma machine
you don't even know who the fuck you are
you pretend
you pretend
you find comfort in lies
while fat cats get rich
off your sweat and toil
open your minds
and let the truth in
open your wallets
and let the moths out
life is short
some of us have paid attention
if you believe in the heaven
you say you believe in
then we know who you are

america
you are a comfortable couch
full of the lost changing of minds
with dust bunnies for souls

a landscape of furniture ghosts
you want to think everything is O.K.
you want to pat norman rockwell or grant wood on the back
it makes it all easier—less painful
a couple of cigarettes, a beer, a paltry wage
and a lotto ticket
america, you are a cheap date

america
you are lost in space
you cage your justice
frame it in grief
where are you?
come out
come out
I am tired of your swindle
tired of your swagger
the man on the corner has a name
the child at the border has a name
carl, we are with you in rockland,
america
go find yourself

Mark Evans
Portugal

Thirst

1. Like my love life, L.A. is in a perpetual state of drought.

It's a crime to water the lawn.

2. Rumors of coyotes overrun the neighborhood.

When they lose their fear of humans, they mingle,
associate people with food, water.

Old Crow - by Alexis Fancher

3. My cat's photo is on a milk carton.

The scattered remains of lost lovers and household pets
litter my dreams

4. *Coyotes have rights, too,* my neighbor says,
when I complain about the carnage. His Chihuahua's leash
hangs on the door.

5. When the famous poet arrived from West Virginia, stood at our sink,
soaped his hands over and over, water gushing out of the tap,
I kept quiet as long as I could.

This is LA, for fuck's sake, I said at last.

6. The white, alpha dog next door is silent for once,
his cohort, the yappy Dachshund, strangely missing.

7. The last time I bathed without guilt, in a full tub of water,
the century had just turned.

Alexis Rhone Fancher
San Pedro, CA

First published in Blood Orange Review, Dec. 2017

My Space Only

The hell I choose
is not for you.
Personal, built
from scratch,
each stone,
each meat hook
fitted in
with years of work
and sweat and blood,
a place to suffer
and be alone,
as significant
as any home
or memory
of one.
There's no room
for two or three.
You will have to find
your own place
in the void
to spend your
eternity.

Joseph Farley
Philadelphia, PA

SCAR CITY

Dogs huddled in the freezing cold
Inhumane.
Homeless passed out on bus benches
Under thin blankets
passed by
like yesterday's trash.

Downtown
too blighted for limos driving by
old wreckage torn down
Residents in affordable shacks
Discard the poor and destitute
We're revitalizing the neighborhood
not you

Real estate sign
for rent for lease
Living space and art loft combo
Very trendy

Lovely green shrubbery
in front of Harbor General
harbors stench of human waste
Bodies guarding precious shopping carts
curl up on sidewalks.
Once a month - $50 a night hotel
sleep, warmth and shower - dignity

Life and death at the hospital
Traumas - swift death
Death lingers for old age and disease.
drug seekers

drinkers of magic elixer
Death by increments

Greenery by 110 North
young scrawny woman
jeans so tight
bare butt shows
rummages in shrubbery
for meager belongings
and bedding

Sunday ads for the garden store -
geraniums and roses
Shop at Macy's and Target
for this season's bedding and clothes.

Make the homeless go away
take the faceless far away
the nameless
the hopeless
the unclean, the outcasts

I don't want to see them
the "them" the "they"
out of sight out of mind
half way houses not in my community
clear the homeless from scant shelter
on benches or in doorways

Take them away
those without jobs or families
those caught up in addictions

elderly outliving usefulness
kicked out of once affordable
apartments
kicked out of once loving families
kicked out for getting too sick and
needy
pushing shopping carts
old women collapsed on sidewalks
drop from exhaustion

it's raining
life is washed away

The rain
falls
splashes hard
on us all

Gwendolyn Fleischer
Torrance, CA

Two by Dennis Formento

Pieces of Osiris

I won't cut my nose off
to spite my face
but they cut this man
to pieces
& took him away
in suitcases
we're not going to sell them
more knives

>   **Dennis Formento**
>   Slidell, LA

Wolves will be wolves

When an accident is planned
what a big accident. What an obstacle
in the sale of heavy weapons

It was an accident. We were asking him questions
when a rogue agent
kissed him goodbye. So
we ordered a paint job after the cleaning lady left

We don't know how this rogue agent infiltrated our crew but
we know that your president
wants to preserve American jobs through arms
& we know nobody gone rogue
will interfere with our business.
Let the killers investigate.
Wolves will be wolves. The severed limbs of Osiris
will gather and reassemble again and again and again.

>   **Dennis Formento**
>   Slidell, LA

Gray Field - by Dennis Formento

Motel Oakland

Sleezy world. Yeah, the bed creaks over my head while some bitchin' whore makes her kill. Another B-grade movie in this Town Lodge Motel Oakland. We're like the out-of-towners, Sandy Dennis and Jack Lemon, only on a *motorcycle* and missing every non-existent campsite on the coast. Dark, cold, wind chaps, bites. Stomach in a knot. No. We'd rather settle for cheap room with a view of Oakland's inner city slime.

Thought I was done puttin' up with this shit when I left my fucked up job. Proofreader at the Rocky Mountain Oyster and all. What's the point? Seems to be it's everywhere. Stress. Tension. Anger. *Perversion*. My mind's been twisted, head nearly yanked from my shoulders as I tried to look beyond the pain I felt inside. Tears streaming in my helmet. A little voice inside becomes consistent echo, cries "Take me home. Feed me. Make me warm. Cuddle me. *Love* me."

This trip has been a trip alright. Blasting through beauty in our BMW space capsule at such a pace and with ferocious wind hammering our streamline out of shape, we have but fleeting instants to fly through.We're on a metal craft in a wind tunnel. The beauty hails down. We clutch for the chance to absorb more than moments of its precious moisture. It beads up on our surface- there to see but not to touch. All rolls off us, falls around, penetrates with force, a confusing turmoil while the peace we cannot soak is left behind.

And now, a bed creaks over my head. I heard the heels clacking up cement stairs beside our door. Harsh woman with a Tina Turner voice is laughing, shrewdly, teasing. Telling the man whose voice beside hers cuts through an avenue of all-night traffic that "he'll get what he paid for but what he wants costs dollars more." That, followed by door slam, followed by bed grating on the floor, accompanied by a subtle sickening scent on this bedspread I lie under, spins nausea through my head and down my gut. My man sleeps, unaffected, by my side. A day of handling his bike with me and luggage on the back across miles of rugged coastline, miles of inner-city terrain, then Tokyo dinner and a quart of beer, has put...him...out. He's not conscious of my suffering. And if he was, he'd say I shouldn't.

I don't know what gives me the sensitivity I travel with. Sometimes I wish I could leave it at home. I want my island in the sun. I want to feel warmed on my skin and in my heart. Warmed by what surrounds me. I reach for a pack of cigarettes. Fill my head with smoke to avoid the filthy noise outside myself. And now I miss the cow that mooed to wake us up two mornings ago. And the blackbird that sang on creekbed all night long. And the pounding sea waves against coastline. I wonder why, when two people first fall in love, they want to hold each other all night long and then, as time goes by, sleep can find them drifted apart.

I want to *shake us awake...*
while a whore and her john
shake a bed overhead...
and somewhere
the sea crashes
on coastline.

Roseanna Frechette
Denver, CO

A Late Night Report

The Terrace Room
eyes over the fat side
of the Oakland's lake
lights –
quiver
blink
like they had a secret
they didn't want to keep.

Under the table
stilettos
needing a walk.
She took them
for a spin
drinks and a kiss.

The cabby was blind
the ride home
cheap
the kiss, a bit more.
They both lasted
about the same
(the cab ride and the kiss)
until the stilettos
came off
and the cab's taillights
crossed East 14th.

The moon checked out
early
was a shit of a night
no one saw its face.

It was one of those
"take what you brought"
kind of nights.
If you didn't bring anything
that's what you went home with
nothing.

The fog
damp
a chill
not a good night for lovers
or stranger.
A few tried
most woke up
lonely.
It was better
that way.
Believe me
I was there.

Bill Gainer
Grass Valley, CA

SANCTUARY

If man in folly forgets himself
let there be somewhere black earth,
pure water and the unsullied skies
of Eden

let there be a refuge for every
animal thought extinct, a hidden
valley, forgotten in a forest
where auroch live unperturbed,
where black rhinocerous wander
in the veldt, or the Malabar civet
hunts prey in Western Ghat

and let Eastern cougars be
welcomed home, the thylacine
be photo-snapped without losing
his stripes, let passenger pigeons
take flight again, replicating
the condor's comeback

and let the mammoth be reborn
to renew the tundra, the frilled shark rise
from deep-sea chasms, the ivory-billed
woodpecker tap its code, the Dodo
bring smiles to children

And who would not be awestruck by
Irish Elk seven feet tall at the shoulders
its antlers twelve feet wide, or not be amused
by a blob fish ugly, yet true to its name

let us share our planet's plenitude
before Paradise is lost

William Scott Galasso
Laguna Woods, CA

MEMORIES

As I lie in bed in complete darkness,
memories of my mom begin to pour
out of my brain like a torrential rain.
As the memories become more tangible,
cold tears begin to roll down
my warm cheeks and into my soft pillow,
and a soft cry escapes my lungs,
and I hear my mother's voice in mine.
My tears become heavier with pain
and moisten my pillow even more,
as my mind travels to a seemingly
forgotten past
as I recognize my mother's voice;
a voice I had forgotten
but want to listen to again.
I look around and search for mom
in the dark, but she's no where,
and I think about my daughter
and ask if she can hear my voice.
I recall my mother's sad songs
and funny but humble jokes
and wonder what my daughter
recalls of me.
I recall my mother's words of frustration
when she'd scream at animals
that'd destroy her garden and eat
her freshly cooked beans,
and we were left without a meal for the day,
and I wonder if my daughter is hungry
but hope she isn't,
and I go back to sleep and recall
more memories of mom
and let my tears become a stream
because tears abound
and don't drown memories.

Martina R. Gallegos
Oxnard, CA

Support Your Local Poet

Adolf Hitler
was an aspiring artist,
twice rejected by the
Vienna Academy of Art,
before he entered
into a career
in politics.

Charles Manson
had a folk-rock band,
and one of his songs
even made it
to number seventeen
on the charts,
but his music career
never exactly took off,
and he found
a new vocation.

In other words,
when your neighbor tells you
he's a painter,
a poet,
a playwright,

pretend
to be interested.

The life you save
could very well
be your own.

Matt Galletta
Delmar, NY

Uncle

C'mon say it
haven't you had enough?
this has gone on for years
I'm not going anywhere
I'll block you at every turn
there'll always be a delay
I'll give you some reason
to not follow through
I'll convince you to put it off
there'll be an excuse to not do it
I'll trick you and lead you to think
maybe tomorrow,
or give you some other
false promise or glimmer of hope
off in the distance
That's how I fool you
again and again and again
I'm not going anywhere
I'll always be right here
obstinate and in your way
wrestling you to the ground
so why don't you just say it
and get over it?
You're never going to do it
it'll always be just out of reach
so why not just give up?
wouldn't that feel better?
what's to lose?
your sense of self?
is it really worth all that much?
C'mon, let's be done with this
Say it.

James Gould
Santa Fe, NM

Night Bound

Patchouli drums my senses
into an empty golden cage
where my rage flutters and settles
amid dreams tossed about long ago.
I can't die without soaring.

Wait —
I remember the embrace or was it a kiss,
summer,
too brief to mean something or
nothing, but the rains came.
The rains came,
and I was stuck deep in an
insignificant mound of overcast days
without two hearts to bleed together.
Oh, what ecstasy the folly of youth enjoys.

Wait —
I remember It was more than just the smile,
the voice,
the glance,
but the eyes which closed at dawn,
never danced with me.

Lorraine Gow
Laguna Woods, CA

I Tried to Hate Boulder

I did—I really tried
Hard
on the ride up to that dumbass college town
NW of Denver
Not my president, huh?
We'll see about that….

I tried to hate Boulder
Fuckin neoliberal nincompoops
Maybe I should bring my .38 up there
and make em dance
like in an old-time western movie…

I tried to hate Boulder
growling on the ride
all the way up from Denver
a whole half hour of rage
Dumb worthless hammerheaded bastards
that always want it their way all the fuckin time!

But when I got up there
and actually saw them…
They're running around real fast
Their eyes are open real big
They got plans
They got dreams
They got schemes
And so, I had no alternative…
but to jump right in.

I tried to hate Boulder
with all my might
Honest to God
I did my damndest
But I just liked the young people too much
Couldn't help it.

Ken Greenley
Denver, CO

Adorned with Benevolence

I have never craved you
Smacked by your beliefs—
the Christ within you,
your family, small children
Are they twins?

We've met for cappuccino
Ate Italian submarines together
I drove your first Tesla,
you drove mine

We talk shop,
humanity, relationships,
clean technology
The future of this stripped earth
manifested by the children
you and your god created

Your kindness is observed
Your faith, broadcast at the
conclusion of each email
you send

I've not wanted you,
knowing we are so different
knowing you are loved
needed
wanted by others you have chosen

But I dreamed of you last night
And woke invoking your pale, holy arms
around me

Friday Gretchen
Ventura, CA

All About Rain—Or Not

that patters on the roof
and windows while an
angry sky brushes the
dusty glass

that pings off the
sides of a rusted
cistern offers a
scant cupful of
bitter water dark
and slick in my mouth.

that searches for life
in a sterile riverbed
ah
where the miracle
where the resurrection

Kathleen Goldman
Manhattan Beach, CA

Disbelief

A man perished in the heat of sport;
my buddy Dan revived him play by play,
cursing the news reportage for giving
his short-lived hero short shrift.

The dead athlete hadn't made page one;
there, instead, was a soldier who died
at an equally callow age: twenty-five-ish,
but in a less indulgent, more selfless
line of duty, implied by wave after wave
of broadcast coverage, imbuing him with
a bravery roadside explosives prohibit.

This candied account of a bitter end,
his reduction to media fodder, iconic,
ultimate sacrifice, their ongoing cycle,
covered it over and over, until we both
sought cover and at length, saw the fatal
encounter as a relatively dull flash
in his never-to-be autobiography.

Worth less alive than resurrected
by sponsors, for an afterlife as bellicose
poster child, sure to shave a few bucks
off the national hate-your-foreign foe
budget and the costly posture of caring:
through a soft lens, their in-depth,
up to the minute familial suffering.

A throng's eye view, between truck adds
and plugs from other hucksters,
our network ventriloquist propped
them up in a syndicated puppet show.

Bad stuff; still worse to be sucked
in by it: invisible millions drawn into
a vacuum hose; too late for those
microbes but not for kinfolk to reread
the doubt and fear between lines
in his letters; now it's all fate, eternity,
pontiffs in robes, a flag-draped affair.

Get up you mischievous corpse, out
from under the etiquette, break through
the blue tarps, shake off your medals,
dirt, flowers of the forest, previously
unworn shirt, mortician's makeup
epitaph, epaulette, gold piping, pipe,
drum and bugle band, bold print obit.

Let the infertile imagination yield a bit,
question your end, flesh out your name,
beyond production, screen projection,
that it not be your last or anybody's
lasting impression, least of all Dan,
my football fan, war veteran friend.

Killers throughout history have killed
with abstract vagary, myth, mystification,
turgid liturgy; no need for detonating
intonation or explosive rhetorical device;
they'll disappear you, kill you twice
and make it appear that you never were.

Tomorrow's reveille will be without
revelation; we'll spend another day or so
in grief and the suspension of critique;
disbelief though, we cannot suspend.

Tom Gannon Hamilton
Toronto, ON. Canada

we are made in her image

I.
we are made in her image

on her horizon a supernova red and orange   explodes into black emptiness with concentric circles
lips of flame with erupting vapor violent in its birth   draw together particles born from the big
bang a whirl of existence expanding   into the dark mouth of the universe

out of space life comes to earth   a visitor in the form of bacteria on a meteorite   that pierces our
planet sperm planted in the watery womb of earth   nurtured by warmth from her lava core carries
the secret of space birthing form   and gaia is born

made of fire and smoldering stone   she emerges from water her black hair aflame   lips soft with
her first breath of compassion her eyes gaze upon her creation   while one arm holds her child a
dolphin clothed in sea-foam fish leap at her feet frolicking in the current of life   white egrets fly
against crimson sky   while we as tiny embryos soon to be born   turn in her belly

II.

gaia   within you lives our creation story of emergence on this planet cooling into blue   erupting
center of magma shifting plates of earth and stone to form other continents and cultures   other
stories and forms

while we humans take penetrating steps upon the earth   in our greed and arrogance we hold
dominion forgetting our brother and sister   the wolf and coyote in our savagery we crush human
bodies destroying traditions unlike our own   forgetting our one mother who gave us form
forgetting our source of dark matter from which we were born

now   gaia your breath of destruction rages   in the black cloud of our greed for oil and power
swallowing coastlines crumbling cities confusing the bees snatching species from the chain of life

we are made in your image   gaia

my heart's question is

are your children to survive

Vijali Hamilton
Santa Fe, NM

BLACK HOLES MATTER...*by Darth N. Vader*

A Black Hole's matter is incredibly dense
Creating an inescapable gravity fence
From which nothing can get out— not even light
Might as well give it up, don't bother to fight.

Through a singularity across an eventful horizon
Why waste a dime for 9-1-1 on your wireless Verizon?
Black Holes matter because they've got a whole lot of mass
Their spacetime distortion is going to kick you in the ass!

Black Holes matter, suck it up like a good Marine
Once they come to town they tend to stay there on the scene
They will drink your milkshake from a distance not in Plainview
When they finish with their firsties you'll be course two.

Black Holes matter 'cause they like to grow much fatter
By stealing your lunch money and then eating your platter
Heisenberg is certain that they cannot be observed
For whatever they take in is going to be conserved.

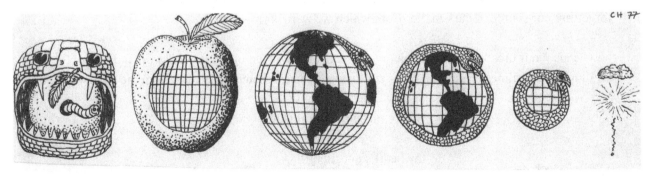

Ourobouros - by Charles Harmon

An ideal black body emitting zero radiation
They can even suck in light, let alone your space station
A Black Hole sometimes spits, let's call it Hawking radiation
If it hits you in the face, you'll get some serious edification.

In curving spacetime no beam of sunshine ever gets out of line
Bottled up, allowed to age, like fine wine for a long time
The more that they eat the more they flow and blow and crow and grow
But "Say it ain't so, Joe!" you know that they will never show a glow.

Black Holes really matter and if you don't agree
You're a deplorable racist without a Ph.D.
You are no ass-trophysicist—just a common asshole
Who I'm gonna flush straight down the cosmic toilet bowl.

E equals emcee squared said Albert Einstein years ago
Yet what it signifies most people really do not know
But when your spaceship's getting pulled in by my tractor beam
You'll find my Death Star's just a Black Hole in a waking dream!

The more matter that I grab and rip apart and gulp and eat
The more power I can gain to always be in the driver's seat!
So if you're finally ready to come over to the darth side
Jump in, sit down, hold on for dear life, get ready for a wild ride!

Charles Harmon
Whittier, CA

II. The month Tom was taken to an Alzheimer's "home"

If it wasn't for bad luck I wouldn't have no luck at all
Abert King, "Born Under a Bad Sign"

Would I be grieving less if
he'd died? At least it
would mean that he wasn't
suffering or hating himself for
the sins of his sickness: The bad
creature that crawls up at dusk. As luck
would have it, I got weak as a baby

and went limp. Otherwise I'd
have fought back. I might have
died or – No.
just a split lip and greening bruises. With luck
nothing's forever. Still I cringe at
sayings like "He's in a better place" and all.

Clarinda Harriss
Baltimore, MD

---

from her new book Innumerable Moons (Beignet Books, 2019)
w/ illustrations by Peter Bruun

Sign of the Crab

In the violent myth
of Cancer, Heracles
wrestled the nine-
headed Hydra.
He wrapped his arms
around the moving
necks tighter and harder
before new heads grew.
A crab sneaked by
and bit his foot.
The warrior crushed it
as if putting out
a burning weed.

Hera tossed the shell
to the stars
in the Grecian sky.

Cancer crosses above
my dark Julys.
A birthday can threaten
like a lost key,
a toppling bookcase
or a wreck on the road.
Hydras spring up daily
and they all keep
coming. Cancers under-

estimate their enemies.
Beasts hulk over them.
If there's any question
about the progress
of my stars, I consult
my daily horoscope:
"CANCER:
Promote your agenda
and don't fall
on your sword."
Crabs are quiet souls.
We don't recall
mythic battles
of our antiquities.

Sarah Henry
Greensburg, PA

Off-the-Grid

Inspired by the image "Floating" by Betsy Mars

She left a crumpled note,

said she wanted to run away
but she really wanted more light:
a bright beam like a comet to lead
her into the enchanted universe.

Incubated like a duckling in an egg, a swallowtail
in a cocoon, she needed outer space to grow
to find strength in the struggle to break free
to contemplate the Big Dipper and the black holes

Ash - Jackie Joice

lodged in her curious mind.

She severed all roots with an ax.

Yesterday, darkness arrived as the gust of wind
snuffed out all interior lights, all power grids:
no current sparking in outlets,
no sound left in a cell phone.

Her family huddled in the basement,
read a mystery novel by candlelight.
Teeth chattered as the mercury

dropped.

She said she wanted to run away

and three weeks later she did, a homeless
wanderer, dragging second-hand hiking boots,
a canteen, an unlit lantern, and an empty backpack

pressing 'light' on her shoulders.

Debbie Okun Hill
Camlachie, ON. Canada

Reading Sylvia Plath...

"I took a deep breath and listened to the bray of my heart
 I am. I am. I am."
A cup of black tea brewed
Four minutes - water just off
Boil...me and Ms. Plath, "blind twins bitten by bad nature"
Ready to meet the
Fools fueling peril, risk,
Folly and murderous lies.
My God wherever you
Are - if you are- help us,
We nubs of meat
Uncoil this mortal
Twist –I am looking for
That white light probability

Show a sign, be visible.
Part the sea.
Send locust, seraphs
Miracles, music, wine
Tea and biscuits,
Redemption, a Samaritan,
A sonnet, a couplet -
Life vexes us
Straightens our shoulders
Interrupts our game of
Solitaire.

Gil Hagen Hill
San Pedro, CA

Untitled

Sunlight streams through window
casting dark silhouettes on wall
and floor next to one-year-old infant
who sits amazed looking at her hand
and shadow it creates while noting
movement disrupts tiny dust particles
floating in the light

May I learn a lesson from the baby
and persist to wonder at precious
life and beauty around me and not
give darkness the opportunity
to steal it away

Lori Wall-Holloway
Pasadena, CA

---

*First published in 2016 San Gabriel
Valley Poetry Calendar.*

The Spider Diaries: Sirens

Flirt with me, misspell simple words with me.
Expose me as if I were a branch
of lemonflowers come out to come out
into the soupy April which blows
your coat and wears it like a white
zipper gentleman remember when
she reddend up with tears about
to burst like hapless rain gunning but a little
spider no bigger than coffee rings
on a sticky bar rail sings it's nice to
(finally) meet you how I know it's
beautiful too but no more tears from you
my dear I was self-aware
for a brief moment today when Sirens
directly sang at me and began fingering
poetry into the sand while one placed
stones and another someone's bones
into my hand and said teach her to skip them
like the days you're not together.

Alex Johnston
Auburn, NY

Flight - by Jackie Joice

Gateway - by Jackie Joice

El Cacto

In Southern California
my needles are singed, dirty,
and scattered throughout alleys.
My skin is cracked like ancient papyrus.
I continuously thirst for dank baptismal rain
to save my withered
prickly flesh from
damnation.

    Jackie Joice
    Corona, CA

Two by Frank Kearns

Mid-Winter Road Trip

Although the overnight weather report
showed that the coming cold front would stay
up in Colorado for another day

the thin film of snow that drifted
across the streets of Amarillo
told us that Flagstaff was out of the question

So we headed down toward Roswell
hoping for Las Cruces
then onto state route seventy

watching the rain freeze on the road
slowing a little more after every roadside wreck
but still going on

till out on a wide expanse of plain
at a place where a pickup truck was overturned
next to a smashed up Honda

someone else
the highway patrol
had to tell us it was time to stop

had to tell us that some days
there just is no way
to keep on heading west

Frank Kearns
Downey, CA

Road Trip Haiku

Crenshaw
For Nipsy Hussle I confess
all the things
I do not understand

Woodruff Avenue
There's the Pollo Loco where
a young mother was
killed for ten dollars

West of Beaumont
In the twisting canyon
the time has come when I
no longer pass trucks

Twentynine Palms
Is it odd that I have to
drive to the desert
to see the night sky?

Frank Kearns
Downey, CA

Geriatric Celebrity Survivor on Isla Nublar*

"At least there aren't really dinosaurs…"
Cloris Leachman leans toward the seaplane window,
scanning the undulant surf. So Samuel L. Jackson
looks up briefly from the latest Walter Moseley,
"Well that would have made it more of an adventure."
Frank Gehry, too, is surveying the jeweled beachscape,
wondering what relics of shelter might remain
from Jurassic Park, for adaptive reuse and recycling.
"Anybody need OFF?" Liza Minelli projects,
over the whine of descending engines.
Reeking of DEET, Jeff Bridges waves her away
"Not me!" He's ready for anything that comes at 'em.
His daddy would be proud. Dame Maggie Smith
glances from left to right, shifts in her seat,
wonders again what could have possessed her agent
to book her for this plebian enterprise.
The final Harry Potter notwithstanding,
she would prefer to be sipping tea at the Dorchester,
breathing fragrant azaleas from the park.
She is, she feels, the only one unprepared
for the excursion. "Liza," she whispers, "please pass
the insect repellant," and closes her eyes with pleasure
at the foam's cool kiss and scent on the back of her neck.
When she looks down at the jolt that signals landing,
the others are reaching up for backpacks and coats
and only she sees the streak of torchlit airstrip
that ends in a fog-laced clearing and the dark.
"Here and now, boys, here and now," she mutters,
under her breath, quoting Aldous Huxley.
It is, after all, only another Island…

Lalo Kikiriki
Joshua Tree, CA

pilot for a future reality show

What I Think About When I Hear Vinyl Records

Kyong's painting, a circle of piano and violin, brown eyes,
one in the painting, the others on people that I love,
ripples from tossed pebbles in the place where the river pools,
bear prints on the sand where the pond begins,

my native drum and the percussive sounds that it fills the house with,
rings from the steam where water evaporates, a pearly Nautilus
the sound of circular music, a loom, the first clock in a 50's schoolroom,
the entrance to a cave, the brain, an atom,

saying hello in autumn in a ring of aspen as the leaves fall,
like gold coins that make rings around the trees,
a ring on my hand, the child of vinyl- a CD,
someone singing notes to encircle the entire house,

a Halloween jack o lantern, wishes that turn into flying horses, carousels
surrounding the earth as they become a ring around the moon,
loggerhead turtles in the air, a glowing halo evaporating,
playing marbles, playing football, playing roulette,

the first snowball you ever threw, a snow angel
the twelve new earthlike planets scientists just discovered,
a round halo that seems to block the sun
and prevents the very stars from entering,

eyes of ghostfish not completely covered over,
wooden hand mirrors, yellow sunflowers, blue cornflowers,
Snow globes, tennis balls, half forgotten basketball hoops where
you used to play ball with your son when you told him he needed to rest from video

games, the place where lovers pace around, an orange orchard looking for fruit to
eat or throw to each other, crayon scribbles of circles when you remember
your father telling you how hard it is to make a perfect circle,
a Mandela, a host, a penny, the fallen lens from your dark glasses,

the lid on a medicine bottle, a tambourine, a perfectly round black rock,
glass Christmas ornaments where the designs inside bring back memories
zinnias at the end of summer, a green birdbath, a hazelnut
A childs bubbles that cling together, then evaporate,

Pandora's broken compact, the top of my coffee cup,
the apple that caused so much trouble,
my first high school dance, rings a round the rosy,
planetary gravity, the unfolding of the universe, the galaxies,

the images of faces of friends I can almost remember.

Dianne Klammer
Boulder, CO

Two by Maureen Korp

Arizona Cactus

In the desert, saguaro stand
big-armed,
     hard along the road.
Half are dead,
     half will be
in fifty years. Don't cry.
      Keep moving.
No one cries in the desert.
  Dehydration kills.   Keep moving.
    The dead stand still. Keep moving.
      Remember me.

Maureen Korp
Ottawa, ON CAN.

The garden

Flowers are floating off
the trees nearby, their
slender branches
curving
into the last light of day

Quiet. Nothing more
is needed
we can stay here
another hour safely
before dark

Maureen Korp
Ottawa, ON CAN.

Previously published: Ada Aharoni, ed. Anti-Terror and Peace; Israel: IFLAC Word Press, 2016

Monument Valley - Raindog

A Tributary's Tribute

News comes as one needs it;
To a poet comes word
that Mary Oliver has closed her notebook,
has passed the torch now to all the fires she stoked.
Poetry, an alchemy,
A Zen rake over the dulled river stones of language,
Coaxes flint,
spark,
surprise,
recognition,
redemption.

With this news I felt impulse to compose
but found no words, only
Silence—
Teeming and grateful—
Silence,
Where all poetry is born
And where it returns,
along with every poet;
Beloved to beloved.
Wordless, Thunderous Thanks,
O' Wise Flint Dust.

Michou Landon
Santa Fe, NM

Ritual

Little soul, how could I
light a candle for you
after I denied you sight
of the sun, moon and stars?

What good would funeral rites be
and wreaths twined with baby roses
after I uprooted your body
curled up like a fiddlehead?

As for a belated christening,
who can baptise the unnamed?

Little one I aborted
you can't speak to me of prayers,
a tombstone as small as a pebble
or a pilgrimage to a Shinto Shrine*
where elf-sized statues of Jizo,
Protector of unborn and lost infants,
are dressed in red bibs and caps,
grieving parents light incense
with smoke wisps dissolving like breath.

In lieu of a rite of passage
absolving me with ritual amends,
let my heart be your grotto
where I can go on revisiting you
without amen or end.

Donna Langavin
Toronto, ON CAN.

Kiyoizu-Dera Temple: a shrine in Kyoto

You Can't Go Home Again, Umm Jihad

In a whirlwind of zealous fervor,
she changed her name to Umm Jihad
and left home to marry a zealot Muslim.
Her husbands were not the kind
who would take her home for a visit
but the kind who encouraged
her hateful posts to Americans:
Fight with Syria's Jihad! Kill fellow Americans!
Two times, she married the kind of men
who killed and died for their religion.
Beliefs change in the face of war
for each death changes us.
After two husbands died fighting the Jihad,
after the bloody sights of war,
after fighting against all religious rights,
she changed. Death changes us all.
In a fit of remorse
and fear for her young son,
she begged to come home.
Sorrow and regret
over youthful arrogance
replaced zealous fervor
in the face of a violent future.
She wonders: Where will her son live?
How can he mature into a peaceful man,
as he is nurtured with bombs, blood,
and butchered bodies all around him?
Now, she and other women like her
beg to go home.
Not even dual citizenship can save Umm Jihad,
for she chose loyalty to insane Jihadists husbands
who brainwashed her to embrace violence,
murder, and hatred against her own people.
Now, both countries disavow her.
"No!" America and England both tell her,
"You can't come home again."

Never, they said.
Of course, her parents plan
legal appeals for compassion,
or at least beg for leniency
for Umm Jihad's crimes against the State.
For now, what will she do?
Where will she go to live?
No one has compassion
for a "naïve, angry, and arrogant"
nineteen-year-old, as she described
her old, young self. In naïve ignorance,
she left home to fight a war
that was never hers to fight.
Hoda, as she once was named,
was religiously deluded.

She sought to kill her own people
over a misunderstood ideology
that theologians themselves declare
is not a part of true Islam.
Living in America,
how could a young Hoda understand
what Syrian Jihadists really believe?
Now, living in a Kurdish refugee camp,
Hoda has learned that,
"You can't go home again!"

Never!

Laura Munoz-Larbig
Anaheim, CA

Poets in conversation - by Kit Courter

Matterhorn Dream - Charles Harmon

ANGELA CONSOLO MANKIEWICZ POETRY CONTEST WINNERS

THIS YEAR'S JUDGE: ELLARAINE LOCKIE

FIRST PLACE • *$500*

Nancy Shiffrin

At The Museum Of Tolerance

we see pictures of cadavers fields of
corpses bunk beds like chicken coops
oceans of ashes we talk about Hugo Boss
military jackets Mercedes Benz
perpetrators still among us we confront the
extermination of peoples we ask ourselves
how we could go *en masse*, to our doom...
we ask what part of us contains this
murder

we reflect on the meaning of the word
tolerance the ability to accept ideas different
from our own the ability to resist pressure to
endure hardship what I feel when I'm writing
toward something and don't know what it is...
what is new here... what have I not grown up
with a woman confides she was ignorant of
Shoah until she moved from Germany to France
where she had a nervous breakdown learning
you Jews don't hate enough she lectures you
must all be deniers
suddenly all I can tolerate is this walk up hill
beneath a canopy of trees bare roots breaking
the sidewalk sun in the west bleeding out into
the lavender sky and the walk downhill
fruit trees in bloom lacy and pink full moon to the
east high in the fading pale blue lone bee
feeding on a flower I cannot name

Risks

Like Rebecca The Woman might question
The Blessing two nations struggling in
her womb. Esau huge hairy ruddy, he first
out, Isaac clinging to his heel, their births
a *shofar* blast a call... she might ask what
drives brother to kill brother daughters
to whore

The Woman might think of Medea who
murdered her sons to spite a faithless lover or
Andrea Yates, depressed housewife, shoving
each of her five children into the bath water
heaving into mouths, noses, throat, lungs... the
wailing, the silence, the knowing...

The Woman might question Simone de Beauvoir
"it is not in giving but in risking life that is man is
raised above animal that is why superiority...is
accorded not to the sex that brings forth but to the
sex that kills..." The Woman might, herself, do the
work of calving heifer straining against chains
farmer thrusting arms into the silky womb
tugging the legs turning the body... with only a
torch for guidance.

The Woman might take her baby to the
laundry each night watch how the
machine's chug chug soothes his cries She
might grieve her own mother dancing a
broken girlhood before the world
or like Sappho The Woman might just long for
her own virginity though eros whips her as a
storm shaking the boughs of the oak tree and
the man sings beneath her window and the
daughters serve her and the children play at her
feet

Shades Of Blue

Do you ever wonder why The Blues
are sad yet there's a Bluebird of
Happiness

if Language were a beast it would be this violet
Serpent coiling and uncoiling through the
waving grasses cunning baffling tempting Eve to
eat from the Tree of Knowledge of Good and Evil
a matter of Life and Death

and Death matters this steel blue rushing river a pipe
depositing broken bottles plastic bags crumpled tissue
snot and shit undigested griefs course toward the
opening floodgates I sit here alone with notebook and
pen idly contemplating shades of blue teal cerulean
turquoise azure cobalt markers of a spendthrift life
the Light appears once more
The Book of Reckoning the
moving finger in the blue
heat at midday an icy
wrenching weariness I
wonder if it's vain to ask how
much time I have

Clouds - Raindog

A Longing

I wanted to be fog, lifting off water,
drifting over a riverbank of shrubs.
Fog, drenching park benches in moisture,
creeping over a city, its hard angles
in contrast to my soft touch.

I wanted to be like fog, pliant, ever-changing,
yet always itself, true to itself,
misty in a mystical sort of way, as if
in my haze, I were a visualization
of a spiritual force, something from heaven.

Soundless, fog carries itself over landscapes,
through the intricacies of skyscrapers and plazas,
over suburban towns nearly lost, subdued,
in the undulating waves of airborne water.
When fog settles, it creates a peacefulness.

Sometimes silvery, often off-white, opaque
except when so thin shapes and colors
poke through the wettish, foggy ambience.
Cloud-like. Puffed-up. Billowing
like sheets on wind or massive brooding ghosts.

I wanted to be fog stretched out over
Creation,
omniscient, a visible chant like Latin
perpetually ringing in the atmosphere,
viewing all that's worth surveying. But
it never came to pass that I was fog.

I never sang a soothing song
over the plains, the valleys, the hilltops,
coating them all with my elusive beauty.
Maybe I desired too much, craved
what was beyond my right to have.

But it is nonsense to think
only Nature should possess omnipotence.

The Dying Lady

Her guests wondered
how she would feel, appear, act.
Serene as her garden, she sat
surrounded by its sunflowers.
While relatives and friends milled around,
she glowed from her wicker-chair throne,
said tender words to one of them,
then beamed cheer to another,
projected empathy to another and another.

The garden party was sparkling:
her husband's gift to her,
and a present from her grown offspring,
their farewell, without words intruding--
a requiem minus music.
No one complained about the heat
rising from soil and walkway slate.

Soda. Hefty burgers. Corn on the cob.
The sizzle and foam of beer.
This sad occasion was saturated
by the merriment of a July cookout,
its yellow rays and scents of roses,
its grills and entertaining grasshoppers,
its over-eager, wacky bees,
its festive, prolific greenery.
Not knowing whether she noticed the sun
gradually shifting, diminishing its light
bothered friends and family,
like a quiz question difficult to figure out.
She never glanced to the west,
never acknowledged petals closing,
stayed radiant,
as shadows elongated and lingered
across her backyard lawn.

Vigil

Three deaths in three months.
You sit near the telephone,
the landline wires like veins
you depend on for news of life,
or death.
At other times, suspended,
you hover beside hospice beds
as you watch. And wait.

From the hospital room, a weathervane
stands, visible to you,
perched on a near-distant gable.
Maybe all sights that dominate windows
signal important predictions.
The tin mechanism points to a location
close enough to see.
You join hands with the dead and dying
by staring in the metal arrow's direction.

No, you're not crazy to let your mind
fly in the direction of the weathervane.
Like a YouTube addict lured to a screen,
or a pilot bound to a flight pattern,
you can't help being riveted
by destinations sketched in the air,
diagrams meant to be read, deciphered.
Surely by now you are aware
you're a virtuoso of death,
knowing your way around a hospice
the way a pianist understands scales.
Medicare is your nickname,
with an emphasis on care.

THIRD PLACE • *$125*

B. J. Buckley

Hiroshige's Mistress:
Her Pillow Book

i. Full moon tonight, wind.

  Blue shadows of pines sweep the snowy path.

  Your footprints, leading away from me – nothing can erase them.

ii. Owl. More melancholy inquiries in the dark.

  What can I say? I no longer have a name. Snow is falling again.

iii. The moon is drunk on the sweet wine of my body – Why, your empty glass?

  Every maple, flaming pyre – if leaves were tears – wind, crying.

iv. Open blossoms, rain- filled, overflowing –

  scattered on the damp earth, their petals, red, each one a flame –

  across my floor, dropped garments.

v. Why drink wine when you could dip your tongue

  in this red blossom, taste sweetness all night? –

    a little buzzing, like a bee caught in a rose.

vi. The terror of the body (you said once) watching hawkfall at twilight

  into a meadow too far to see more than death's shadow.

  My Hawk, your descent, sharp-beaked, into bloody joy –

  do you deny it? My ravished belly, shattered heart, torn plumage, broken wings

vii. Naked in frosted grass whipped by winds from the south –

  sharp cold lashes: Waiting for fox to come and lap up the salt of my tears.

viii. Remembering you, I long to recall nothing – your love bites hot brands

  on the flesh of my breasts, where you rode me, a red ache –

  A kiss on the head erases memory – pine's icy lips on mine.

  I bend to silver tongues of snow, desiring emptiness.

ix. An empty vessel is already too full – breath, wind – See?

The leaves fall, unread, the moon's a pale stain no laundress can remove.

x. Moonlight tongues my skin where your rough hands caught me in their corded snare,

held – marked me. Loosed, my rabbit-heart pounds, hunter – I dare not move.

xi. That silk dragon who sleeps in your belly – chain me to a stone, call him!

(when he plunges into my dark sea, plunges, breathing fire –)

xii. Moon with her bright ropes binds my wrists, slips silver hands beneath my silks, pauses –

How long will you sit, shadowed, to watch her have her way with me?

xiii. Rain last night. There were geese, honking and calling above the cloud layer.

At sunrise, mist rose from the millrace, wind in the maples – a thousand departing wings.

xiv. When I see dew on a red leaf fallen into the grass, I think –

salt pearls, fire – how each curled edge is a blade.

xv. Yellow soap in a common shower stall – the scent of a man I loved, long ago –

October, my skin slicked with lather – his hands . . .

xvi. My nipples rub against the rough wool of my shirt,

stand up hard and red as the arils of yew.

xvii. Between my legs you were like a horse drinking after a desperate journey.

So rough, your coarse beard – I complained – your thirst was merciless!

Three days ago, and still I throb and sting.

xviii. Yesterday men raked the leaves, today they are burning them.

Last night I, too, was flame.

xix. The moon sank so slowly into the cleft between two mountains –

You entered me –

an eternity, to bend and string the bow.

xx. Spiders have traversed on silken bridges our paths between the aspens.

They break across my face – ghosts of kisses.

After moon-set, on our backs in wet grass, we watched meteors burst

across the heavens. The one that burned hottest I could not see.

xxi. You slept – I moved from your embrace to pillow your head on my open thighs.

The fragrance of night-blooming flowers – perhaps it will enter your dream, awaken you?

xxii. I knew that one day those lessons on tonguing the flute to prolong the note

would serve me well.

Xxiii. These verses are for you, but you have no ear for poetry.

Perhaps I should whisper lines from Wu's treatise on forging swords?

Baked Potatoes Late at Night

Which aren't really because I did them
6 minutes in the nuke which is what
everyone in the west calls the micro-
wave because so many of us live at
ground zero or as close as not to
matter, there are silos everywhere
(the missile kind) you can see them
from the house or the alfalfa field
or the highway and they have
"communication lines" which go
underground and their paths are
marked with reflective orange tape
around the tops of fence posts,
the oversize ones you use in corners
or for a gate, easements on your deed
just like for a phone line or the
electricity, and by "communication
lines" they mean that a computer
somewhere will send a signal to
launch because in tests they found
that even with a gun to his head one
of the two people required to push
the button would just say no, would
refuse, would say not on my soul so
kill me, if I help you we'll all be dead
anyway, 68% of the time, no, just
shoot, so they decided humans are
unreliable and passed the job off
to some computer programmed by,
probably, one of the humans who was
willing to pull the trigger — anyway, the
potatoes, my father was Irish, came
over on the boat with Johnny
Fitzgerald and a leprechaun in a
shoebox, but that's another story
for another time, my father loved
baked potatoes with too much butter

and pepper and too much salt, and he
was an electrician, and when I was a
little girl they sent him away to
Wichita Falls, Texas, to learn how to
wire missile silos, and he did, all over
Wyoming, climbing down deep in
the dark of the earth to make sure
the buttons would work, mutually
assured destruction, even though
he had us, my sister and I, had
children, us who would die first
because we lived in Cheyenne,
Wyoming, with F. E. Warren Air
Force Base and the silos were
everywhere around us, you could
see one from Crystal Lake where
he took us fishing, and from north
of town where we would take drives
to watch huge thunderstorms and
tornadoes spinning across the prairie,
raising dust, they built rich people's
houses out there as the time passed
and every few years those corkscrew
winds blow a few apart, it's just north
of the Base, silos practically in their back
yards, and it's ironic, how I moved
to get away and you can't, here I am
with fields of alfalfa and barley and
lentils and missiles and rapeseed and dill,
just crops — food, fodder, hatred, fear —
(everyone grows their own potatoes,
even though by fall you can buy
hundredweight bags from the Hutterites
for under twenty dollars, some of those
spuds as big as your head, Red Pontiacs,
Russets, Purples, Yukon Golds)

WINTER FIELDS

Fertile, fallow,
rippled furrows frost-filled
foam on currents
outward urgent
towards the leaning
fence, slack wire's surrender,
barbs, the sharper
hoarfrost needles pricking
air – the cold.
Two horses in the drifted uncut
hay lift up their heads, their manes
in braids of ice, thick bodies
blanketed with white, sun-
saddled, smoke
of breathing rising from their
muzzles – then they bend
to graze.

Posts lean akimbo
over grass and dirt, the dark
unplanted field too regular
in emptiness: disk, harrow, plow,
all for nothing. Snow
falling again, the horses bridal
veiled, dark chaste eyes
cast down.

Beyond the fence
the blankness lends itself to story –
dear-leap, heart-hoof
air arc over,
turkey track, coyote scat,
a place where wings made death
an angel for an instant.
Hawk floats effortless on wind
as fallen leaf on icy water.
No failure is too terrible
to be borne,
no absence entire.
The horses are running with their tails lifted
headlong into the storm.

Love and Sorrow

I. So that you will see me my rhymes sometimes shed their skins,
become shadows on warm stone. Adornment, tiny cymbals
for your thighs, juicier than plums.

I watch the skeletons of my verses from so far away that they forget me
to follow you. They become stray dogs, begging for scraps.
At night they sleep on your porch, they twitch in their dreams of you –
it is all your fault that the silk of my hair does not cover them,
that they have fallen out of my mouth.

When I did not know you, they crept up onto my couches.
I grew used to their slumbering heads heavy on my breasts.
I want to teach them to speak on command to you,
I want you to understand the lolling red tongues of their language.

Leashes clipped to their collars tug them away.
The scent storms under bushes excite them to ecstasy.
When they sniff at the crotches of passers by, that's me, in disguise,
oh, sorrow, not you, not you, the worn jeans of strangers, their empty pockets.
Come back, come back as though you had always intended to,
with a stick for a gift, a green ball, a bone.

II. Do you think of me, when you are walking somewhere
along a sidewalk, in shoes with thin soles? When a bird
in its shadowy dress clatters up towards the air, little ship
of feathers, little sails of its wings, towards the sky, do you remember
oceans, how I was the tide, how you were the moon?

I think perhaps your heart has amnesia, though in every city I search
the sad pages of phone books for your name – sad phone books,
all of those numbers unloved by anyone. Some nights I've
dialed them, the secret codes of strangers, pretending –
The park? I say, the Japanese lanterns?
Feeding bread to the gulls on the beach in a gale?

We were young, you've forgotten, but I cannot forget you
in your worn Levis torn out at the knee. There must be a girl
who kept their photographs, fair girls who lost their area codes,
do you think of me,
not knowing it's me you're recalling,
when the phone rings, and someone hangs up before you can say
Hello?

III. You were lost to me when first I opened – flower,
door – What shall I do with the corners of air?
They shimmer like ghosts of your graceful body.
Bright wind of your breath, swallowed by sky,
how shall I lure it away from the clouds, back again into the cage
of your ribs, when you leave the door to it always open?
When we are dust, how will I know which swirling grains
were the soil of you, rich loam, generous field
of your embraces? Salt of the sea, tides of heartbeat,
blood's estuaries, where? Because you have vanished
I take off my skirts, press my body to stones –
There is your heat! My Sun, locked in granite!
Or the spent coolness of your skin, moonlight –
there, there – but you've slipped out
and into the dress of deer, into a coat of dark pines.
Your footprints disappear into thickets of willow,
the branches of willow, yellow and red and thin and bare,
bluest shadows, how quiet is this winter country of your absence.
Little shells, remember! Your ears that I kissed, pink
labyrinths, my lost voice wandering there, my whispers –
Stones, do not forget! Bone's architecture, frame
of the hollow of your palm beneath a breast, snake curve
of your spine in sleep. The skin of pale ice on the pond this morning,
your skin that was ivory and alabaster!
No matter how desperately I exhort the roses
to bloom, to flame up – your lips, your cheeks –
they have stopped paying attention to me. Their petals fall,
they fall, they consort in silence with shattered maple.
How is it that you have melted like early snow?
I would sew up my heart with a thread
of crows, I would mend the worn shoes
of my despair. Oh, beyond starlight, farther than far –
Even the wild geese betray me with their longing!
Aligned to their invisible compass, wild geese calling in darkness.

Norman J. Olson

POETRY II

Teatro Paraguas poets, Santa Fe, NM - Photo by Kit Courter

Two at Portland Museum of Art

Two women stand at windows not far from the sea
in a museum not far from the hospital where
Brother says, "It's time to go to the circus."
My sister calls me from South Philadelphia

as she walks to Center City on New Year's Day
while the Mummers strut Broad Street and Brother
struts the hall to show patients how it's done.
A few days ago he could not even sit up.

The next night she calls at the end of *Criminal Minds*,
asks me to look up the quote they used at the end
about a circus by Charles somebody, last name
she doesn't catch.

In my family there are no accidents, only connections
not yet seen, my sister as intuitive as a Roma reading
your palm, which she's done a time or two.
Her boyfriend's family makes a living that way.

The two paintings at the Portland museum are no accident
either, Yasuo Kuniyaski's nude *After the Bath* with back
to the window onto a port that could be Japan or could be
the rocky coast that Winslow Homer pointed at Black Point.

In Homer's *An Open Window*, the woman faces outward
as if Emily Dickinson contemplating her small world
made large by her words. The paintings are two sides
of the same as I am with Brother.

I started at the sea and left for the Southwest to write.
He sailed the world, then lived the life of the Beats
and hippies and down and outers who populated
the small press in the 80s where I first published.

And I'll damned if he didn't on his deathbed
quote Charles Bukowski, "We're all going to die,
all of us, what a circus!" and then dance
down the hall.

   Kyle Laws
   Pueblo, CO

Why Some People Die Alone

I hear you curse and beat
against the walls of a prison
you've lined with harps, books,
and broken hearts mounted
like trophies on the walls.

Propelled by a mild irritation,
and morbid curiosity, I want
to catch a glimpse of the real you
I've heard quietly weeping
as the sun sinks behind
the skyscrapers in your dreams.

But it's not to be. The first day
I knocked on your door
to welcome you to this limbo
of lost souls, you appeared
wearing nothing but an old pair
of wool long johns and
brandished a spear decorated
with urban tribal designs. My *hello*
tumbled from my lips to the floor.

Since that day, I've never seen
you leave this place, though maybe
you do while I'm asleep. Does it
really matter? We're both here for
the same reason; we'll never say *yes* ...

Marie C. Lecrivain
Los Angeles, CA

My Sister Rides a Sorrow Mule

my sister says she rides a *sorrow* mule
her words
for the beast of burden
saddled by her beau
infertile foal of jack and mare
become the sorrel molly
taking the path of sunlight
striding up through Santa Inez Mountains
by way of California chaparral and woodlands
near Santa Barbara
in the five-million-year-old range
she plods
and I am put in mind
of Balaam's mount balking
at the angel guarding the way
between wall and vineyard in the Book of Numbers
as I think also
of Palm Sunday and the sacred burden
of the gospels
or of *Platero* companion to the poet of Andalusia
or perhaps of Sancho Panza's anonymous donkey

as I remember the woman Georgina
astride her mule calling out joy and sadness
in a shared memory
of mother and father
gone back through time
gone back to the very womb
long before the ovum porous moment
of my own conception
and all
the star burst and occasional truths
come rushing forth
in slow confusion
as it is with first darkness
falling on the farmhouse windows of home
when the ghost maple taps on glass
in the come-clear gloaming
that haunts the world that carries the wind
through the yard
no longer there

John B. Lee
Port Dover, ON Canada

Me and Dad and Jesus

Me watching Me and Dad and Jesus
In a faceless, cake-sliced house
A guillotined exposed-bone Victorian
Planted in the void
It happened so quickly
Dad in the parlor
Jesus shattering a whiskey bottle over his head
Me watching Me and Dad and Jesus
Not knowing, but knowing
Why Christ knocked him out cold
Crack!
The brown liquid Rorschached on the Lamb of God's
glowing white gown
As the jagged glass shrapneled in slow-motion,
filling the room with booze and honky-tonk brawl
My Dad dropped hard to the floor
Like he had been sucker-punched by the Lord
I knew that Jesus had anger issues
Kicking ass and taking names in the Temple
Thought Me watching Me and Dad and Jesus
And you can only turn so many cheeks
Then Me watching Me felt Jesus grab my hand
Whisking me up Jacob's Ladder to the attic

(A dream-encased metaphor for escape
cloaked as heaven, cloaked as an attic
I figured out much later in Psychology 101)
But, Me watching Me and Dad and Jesus
Was just a kid who believed that salvation
and divine retribution were one and the same
And didn't understand such things
As dreams sometimes being stories
We tell ourselves
At night
When days are filled
With nightmares
But I was happy
Ecstatic
Me watching Me and Dad and Jesus
Dad crumpled on the parlor floor
Me watching Me and Jesus ascending to the attic together
Feeling
So Blissful
So Grateful
So Guilty
That Jesus saves
Even sinners like me

   Rick Leddy
   Pasadena, CA

   _____

Published Spectrum 17, Dec 2018

Blame

a woman I never met is banging
on invisible bars to be let out,
I hear it in her eyes, her daughter says
for me to hear it too,
a voice silenced by feeding tubes
and a ventilator

… words only take me so far,
and in truth, I don't want to go
any further than this…I think
about soldiers being taken prisoner
in Iraq or Afghanistan, countries
I've never been to, people put in dark
cells, no idea if they will ever get out
goes on sometimes for years
far from where I am

II.

who is to blame
for taking a woman's life
to prolong it? And have.

The doctor who gave her a year
to live without a new heart valve
the daughter who told them
to go ahead…the woman who
saw the new door open and walked
through it past her 86 years,
just yesterday she'd wrapped days like scarfs
around her, so many she couldn't choose,
breathing in sun like air, confident
there'd be more days now
like these

III.

one long day stretches over weeks
the forecast unchanged:

do you want to live, her daughter asks,
a hoarse voice hauled out by sheer force of will,
live she begs her daughter, no, pleads with her
who misunderstands; a matter of semantics
the banging keeps on, louder now

Linda Lerner
Brooklyn, NY

Urban Squirrels

Agile brown squirrel races down city-blackened
tree trunk, snatches a discarded crust,
then up, up to family leafy nest,
there leaving lunch for Mom and small ones,
off again at breakneck speed, pausing
in a skid, choosing, nipping at branchlets,
twigs fan a duster-like cluster of spring pale leaves,
snap and he's off, up, up - with more nesting material -
enlarging their treetop home.

  Dashing across waving branches, leaping from
tree to neighbouring tree - maples,   until
each perfect fuzzy new twig is located
and placed in their home, woven strong against
spring showers and unruly gusts.

        A three metre high fortress, almost softening
sirens of fire trucks - snug against the weather,
safe from earth-bound predators, those off leash hairy pets,
Mom watches skyward for flying enemies:
hawks by day, owls by moonlit night.

Little creamy babes aloft -- cuddle close --
sharing Mom's warmth and milk,
dreaming of their turn to scamper up/down for treasures,
leap between tall trees like Dad, natural circus performers,
mix of high wire devilry and ballet precision.

Roaming below are furless giants - who rest on metal
benches, lunching and leaving good bites, crunchy crumbs,
then brave Dad snatches a Big Mac Pac, nearly flattened,
smells of grease, rarely tasty nuts, yet then up,
up -- with this huge and ready-made wall unit,
until at the last lunge to flip supper inside the nest;
it slips free and flutters back to the pavement.
Dad begins another search...

Bernice Lever
Bowen Island, BC CAN.

Afternoon by the River

I want to tell the whole story about my father…
to show what happened to him––why he had rages.
His story keeps coming out in prose.
I want it to be a poem.

I imagine the weather that day,
autumn sun and wind in their hair––
they are riding in a convertible,
just come from the horse races
on Yom Kippur––
a man, his beloved wife, and favorite uncle.
I imagine them in high spirits, kibbitzing.
Life is good.

Then the unimaginable happens.
I want to tell how a drunk on the wrong side
of the road….

A head-on collision.
His wife and uncle
killed instantly. He
is in a coma for two weeks.

He wakes up to all that loss

with a steel plate in his head
pressing on a part of the brain
that gives him migraine headaches
and brain damaged rages
for life.

My father wrote a poem about it:
The sun went out that day
in a diary entry.

His son is a year and a half old.

I want to tell how decades later
his sister Helen murmurs:
He was never like that before the accident.

~~~

Almost ninety years later,
I sit in tall grass by a river listening
to it sing, watching its swirls
and eddies, the turns in its course––
seeing how a river finds its way
around rocks and logs, clogged debris,
how it rivers new pathways
of ongoingness.

My father remarried…and married again.

His second marriage, to a beautiful woman
named Mavis, he had annulled:
She was tubercular.
A Darwin enthusiast, he believed
in survival of the fittest…Did not want
his four-year-old son exposed.
Those were his words.

Pausing at a photo of her in a family album,
did he not also tell me she was pregnant?…
by someone else?

Barry and I are the children of his third marriage.

If you––or I––want more,
ask the river.

Jane Lipman
Tesuque, NM

Six Million Feet High

Delta flight 403
London to Vienna

Row 13 seats A and B
Mother and me

Seat C
Austrian man
Telling mother that
Holocaust did not happen

"Es war nicht," he says in German

Czech mother
War survivor

Stands up and blurts out
Her best German

"Es war und es war sehr schlecht"

The slaughter took place and
Was very bad, she says

Finally free
Without apathy
Mother sits down
In B

I stop shaking knee
Order hot tea

Radomir Vojtech Luza
North Hollywood, CA

*Published in the Shoah Remembrance issue
of Poetry Super Highway (2018)*

Trump Card

i wasn't surprised
when Trump was elected president.
angry,
inflamed with rage, maybe,
with fear for the future, maybe,
but not surprised –
after all,
what more poetic an image possible
to confirm, tag & time
the official death of The American Dream?
& now, almost a year in
& despite everything
i still don't wish for impeachment,
not assassination or coup,
nothing deadly or bloody,
no – i wish for the exact opposite.
i wish for a Trump awakening.
a Trump metanoia.
a knockout blast of godhead & revelation
illuminating the Trump body & mind.
after all,
what more poetic an image possible
to confirm & time
the resurrection of Life

from the corporate death-grip
of Absolute Capitalism
than a few long & dark,
deep nights of the Trump soul
into a sacred & psilocybic
humble & heart-centered transformation?
an expansion of consciousness?
The Hero's Myth on the grandest scale?
& who a more perfect candidate
for Buddhahood
then the one at the very top?
just the possible jolt it would serve
to the larger psyche. . .
the discovery of aliens
tomorrow morning
could not be more important
unexpected or beautiful,
more meaningful, even,
than a visionary shamanic soul retrieval
in the highest office
of the land

Mike Mahoney
Wallingford, PA

Two by Georgia Santa Maria

Winter Seduction: To a Graveyard in Scotland

Viscous snows against the runes
obscuring the gravestones,
markers, names of the dead.
The very fence of iron, black,
accents the pattern that is
its own surround—a crow takes flight.
These generations lost,
to history first, then time.
Even their own won't recognize them;
the unlit candle cold within the church,
darker than the snow outside,
mounting on the slated tile roof,
the river clogged with ice.
There is a silence,
but for the rook above,
who breaks it open with his cries.
All winter courts us to its side,
seduces with its quiet white.
We will succumb, become the bride,
embrace the stones, and die.

Georgia Santa Maria
Albuquerque, NM

Dust Devil

Dust Devil, I mistook you
for a full tornado;
you were over before I knew.
I watched you, then,
out across the landscape,
kicking up the
friendly tumbleweeds,
gum wrappers,
sand-papering the skin
of everyone
that knew you—
then disappearing
like a wisp,
against the mountain's
distant blue.

Georgia Santa Maria
Albuquerque, NM

La Lluvia Bar

when the rails are wet,
when the grass is green,

when lovers we regret to have not known better
rise up from the dead -

when crickets give recognizable signals,
when you find letters that were missing for fifty years -

when you lick a painting and it tastes good,
when the circus comes to town and a poet is in charge -

la lluvia bar will open
and its doorbell will sound like a waterfall.

exhausted 'sluts' from the old city
will sit themselves down, comb their hair

and each other's but not yours.
all drinks will quiver in their clear glass bottles;

an old man will sweep
moths from the four corners

and rain will rule and rain will rule,
and every tree will grow a foot

between the hour of despair
and the first point of dawn.

Mary McGinnis
Santa Fe, NM

Ministers of Roofing

Dawn just breaking, vehicles converge on my street,
the plates say Chihuahua, Sonora, Santa Fe.

The crew gathers. Dark pants, black kneepads. Gray hoodies are pulled up,
caps brim-backwards. The guys toss coffee cups and close the phones.

Boots rise in front of my kitchen window, mounting the red extension-ladder
rung by rung and, like balloons, disappear on high.

I hear orders barked between men whose faces I can no longer see.
Shovels overhead batter at the gravel, as if beating out a fire.

I'm at my desk when part of the ceiling caves in and clouds cross the hole.
Debris and Spanish curses filter through the gap and settle on the mantelpiece.

How little thought I've given to the roof ! It's been a gaping absence
in my count of blessings, this layer that marks my rooms off from sky.

Now the upended wheelbarrow drops the old roof bit by bit into the dumpster.
Now the crew dresses the deck in fresh tarpaper out to the parapets.

The drama's at its height. Foreman Ruben and red-gloved Marco, handlers
of the fire-dragon, put blowtorch to bitumen, then stomp it while it's hot.

They generate an asphalt spell to keep sun and snow
away from me, my fireplace and all I treasure.

The odor of tar pervades the space. I love the ritual,
and I begin to love the roof that covers me.

Basia Miller
Santa Fe, NM

Previously published in the Santa Fe Reporter, March 21, 2019

A Widower's Morning

Wake up.   Get out of bed.
Open the curtains.   Raise the shades.
Go to the bathroom.   Shave.   Strip down.
Shower.   Dress.   Take blood pressure.
       Check blood sugar.

Go to the kitchen.   Look at pigeons,
Scratching.   Pecking.
Drink juice.   Eat cereal.
Make coffee.   Open
            shut the frig.

Turn on TV.   Listen to news.
Turn off TV.   Sit on the Lazy Boy.
Read stories.   Move to my wife's picture.
Pass my hand over it.

I miss rubbing her feet.   Miss our morning walks.
Wall shadows fade.   The attic creaks.
Trying to remember,   I pace
room to room.   Look out the window.
            Look in the mirror.

Looking for something, I'm upset
because I can't remember.   Stand still.
Turn left/right.   Brightening the house,
the day reveals the inescapable,
            vacant distance.

Joseph Milosch
Poway, CA

Quite Contrary

When we were kids, every house had eeny meeny offspring
who played outside past dark
with no one to Wee Willie us into bed.

Mom and Dad drank daquiris and ate deviled eggs
in the TV room full of number games:
nightly reports of enemies, allies, body counts.

Regular as dickory dock
the little dog yapped all night.
Dad tied him to the hose bib,
yelled *shut the hell up*,
and next morning found the dog hung by his leash
over the six-foot fence, ding dong dead.

Our baby sitter read us rhymes
then ran away with Dad like hey diddle diddle.
Mom stood alone.
Heigh-ho, the derry-o.

Babies, doggies, daddies, wives.
Every evening we saw them with kitchen knives
weeding crabgrass from the bluebell beds.

Uptown and downtown,
inside their chain-linked yards
the ladies muttered:

--*when the boys came out to play*
--*the cupboard was bare*
-- *the ants go marching*

And one by one, the children, we all fell down.

Elaine Mintzer
Manhattan Beach, CA

These bones

Walls shape a goddess
that has never known
day. Or night. Blind mole
groping to read
this Braille universe.

Chorus:

I have carried
these bones for
as long as I can.

Bleach-white crows,
eyes lightless,
feet imbedded, wings derailed.
Black beaks that
chip into the heart
of the unsuspecting.

Chorus:

I have carried
these bones for
as long as I dare.

Alabaster city
carved from the tusks
of unguent mountains.
Deep beneath a rosette sky
that has never known sky
a wind that whistles
tales of the outer world.

Chorus:

I have carried
these bones as
far as they will allow.

Michael Mirolla
Oakville, ONT. CAN.

Dead Bird - Kit Courter

Two by Tony Moffeit

A Woman With No Arms

i am something
and its opposite
i am two
the space beneath the dream
the skeleton of thought
puppets and mirrors and masks
everything is perfect
time is waiting in the wind
i am a woman with no arms
i play the guitar with my feet

i refuse to be broken
fingers of wind palms of sleep
and in their moving a landscape
of bones so today the dust is
moist and there exists a
rhythm that rises like mist
a feeling of bones dissolving
in the earth

i am a woman with no arms
i learned to drive with my feet
what is it we can do
a tongue to speak in
what you want me to do
in the broken down light
to face the night
let's dance on a dark star

i have found the secret
of turning toes
into fingers
reversing
the order of things

i refuse to be broken
like pieces of a mosaic
reassembled again
in a geometry of resurrection

let me hold you
with my invisible arms
a regeneration of love
i seek the impossible

Tony Moffeit
Pueblo, CO

Tattoos Don't Cover All the Scars

one thing at a time
he said
the large man sitting next to me
on a bench
with his walker and oxygen tank
tattoos running up and down his arms
both of us waiting for rides
it's like dying and coming to life again
every day
he said
i had no idea nor interest
in what he was talking about
and his voice grew louder
as he told me about his afflictions
and i won't tell you what he said
only that he said it
in a loud voice
and he would not stop
i was getting sick to my stomach
listening to assortment after assortment
of ailments procedures rare diseases
and cures worse than diseases
and all i could think was
ride ride please come

but as he shifted into the next tale of his conditions
i thought
i need to concentrate on something else
and channel out his monologue
so i focused on the tattoos
on both his arms covering scars
if you looked closely you
could see the lines of the scars
had become a part of the tattoos
when the man said
one more thing
and it was one of those
moments when you have to choose
between running
or listening to one more line
of an exhausting diatribe
i chose to listen:
i swore that if i ever got this bad
i would take a gun and shoot myself
but now that i'm here
all i care about
is waking up tomorrow

Tony Moffeit
Pueblo, CO

Ukrainian Daughter's Dance

"You love Saskatoon
love Saskatchewan
proud to be Canadian
you're just a Ukrainian prairie girl?"
my daughter, Natasha recants

"I am what I am" I say
I bleed green for the Saskatchewan Roughriders
Grew up on a farm near Hanley/Kenaston
love winter wind in my hair
love breathing in the prairie sun
love changing of autumn leaves
love red sunsets, sparkle of northern lights
love gardening in the rich soil
dancing barefoot in the black earth

I'll always be a prairie girl
and daughter of a Ukrainian matya

A leopard has spots
Zebra stripes
Farm girl loves nature

And a Ukrainian Prairie daughter will always
dance barefoot in the black earth

Marion Mutalla
Saskatoon, SK. CAN.

Cheering for the Trees

I want the trees to take it all back
Whether the earth wants to push up new continents
Or become the smoothest sphere sanded by wind and flood
Neither ice nor Eden for a blanket
I want the marks and fissures to balance out
And the tallest come back to rule
I want the ingredients back to make it come true
Air and earth free of the killing acid, salt and heat
Water fresh and pure cycling around the planet
Let my bones nourish the tallest
Or even the sprouts of the giants
That and that alone gives the lie shame
The loudest defilers were to have dominion
For the greatest inhabitants never made a sound
Except for their dying fall
Their last imprint on my existence
I want the quiet towering giants
To take it all back
Turning to unbothered stone in their own time

Evan Myquest
Sacramento, CA

Margaret Atwood Rewrites Dreiser

You row out to the middle of the lake
where the moss grows thick
and in the distance
you hear the motor of his boat
coming toward you.

You grit your teeth
can almost see him in all his scars,
tall and hairy, leaning toward you
as you row away,
and the faster you row
the louder his engine gets
until he is up
next to you, all hum and grin
that used to excite you.

You don't want him
to know how you love it
out here alone

how you love the moss
and celebrate fish leaping.
He cuts the engine,
rows up close,
holds his camera to his eye —
Hey, how 'bout a photo?
He says he's nostalgic,
wants to touch you
just one more time . . .

But you're not a cat.
You lick your fingers
smooth your legs
lift up a paddle.
He aims.
You smile, and laughing
he says, That's it,
just as you raise the oar
high above his head.

Linda Neal
Redondo Beach, CA

_____

Published by Bloodroot, Spring 2019

post-mfa horror story

Halloween arrives
and I'm living with my mother
[rent-free]
until I can find a job;
of course,
"rent-free" doesn't mean
totally off the hook;
she needs
help with household chores,
help with the yard,
help with various errands—
Today she gives me her Visa card
and
a grocery list: "Feel free,"
she says, "to get a little something
for yourself . . ."
So I'm off to Kroger,
torn between plastic vampire teeth
and
a tube of fake blood.

    Ben Newell
    Brandon, MS

What She Told the River

I will lay down my rings for your transport fee
and borrow your blue for a rucksack

Make of my journey a wet undoing:
Hang my dress like a mast on your sunken harvest
Bedeck your mud-stuck schooner

Dance with my slippers
and blend my voice with those of your silent floaters

Make my skin wear the coolness of fishes

Scribble a new story on my face
and let minnows feast on my eyes

Have birches bow their shaggy heads
to note my slow erasure

Thread my bones with your fingers, play me
like a long-lost harp

Then, sew me to the sea.

    Terri Niccum
    Buena Park, CA

America, Again

america, again
your vigor tests my soul.
are you the beautiful lady or
the vampire that sucks my blood or
are you both, for
i am the son of the son of the jew
who ran for his life & now am i best
to be preparing to run again?
i look at the black man, the latino man,
the middle eastern man, the gay man &
we ask ourselves should we
be boarding up our windows forth
the coming of the rocks?
will there be a shooting in the night?
fires in the sky? kristallnacht all
over america?
my life has begun it's slow ebb.
in the distance I hear the children chanting.
i listen carefully for their words.

> **normal**   Aug/2018
> Saugerties, NY

An Hour is a Minute, or Vice Versa

In the intrepid hour I wake to pee,
or drink water climate change
will make holy, I first pause
to converse with toes quibbling
sharp objects protruding like rebars,
irregular lines redrawing into forms,
and forms into shapes I think I know.
How is it different, if we sleep, or stare
as wolves into the olive-colored dusk?
Either way, Planck tells us, the backyard
erodes away incrementally, cratering
otherwise familiar contours of cohesion.
And while you stargaze, lavishly in bliss,
visitors from Farout ride in, one by one
on aerocycles powered by cosmic dust,
to graciously fill it in, like granted wishes.
Who can discern a mouse from a snore?
Who rests, and who stands on guard?
The night is long, the sky is dark as oil,
morning stretches toward a quantum shore
like uninterrupted footprints in the sand.

> **Edward Nudelman**
> Seattle, WA

Paul Bunyan Tales

they always call me Reno
and I was born in Vegas
I grew up in Tahoe
went to school in Truckee
didn't have a father had a mother
some say I'm an asshole
maybe I am but I'm a big tipper

never finished high school
never thought of college
took a typing class at night school
get my GED
I still call Rite Aid Thrifty
I call a Nissan Datsun
my real name is Blackie
I had a cat named Breadcrumb
I used to run with outlaws
now I just run

I had a job in Carson City
Hammond organ salesman
I'd demonstrate the keyboard
and I'd sing along
they fired me for stealing
I did a little jail time
I took a stack of C-notes
the fuck, it was written in the song

I met this girl in Quincy
she took my hand in marriage
her name was Becky
we tried to make a family
we wanted many offspring
but we only got two sons

I believed she'd up and leave me
least I thought she'd try to
after the accident with the little one
but she stayed on with me, wouldn't go

we moved to Lassen County
bought a house in Westwood
I worked at Red River Lumber
as a cherry wood steamer
our son Chet was quite the rebel
tiny Lyle died of crib death
all though Chet never knew his brother
he still loved him his whole life

Chet moved north to Shasta
made a new life his own now
found a nice gal Beth to live with
they had no desire to marry
they had no desire for children
they set their minds to love each other
held each others hands all the time
they lived for one another
nothing else mattered
their love didn't diminish
it multiplied it multiplied
unafflicted unopposed
unhallowed
and it multiplied
and it multiplied
and it multiplied
that's how it was all their days

John Pappas
Long Beach, CA

Two by Jeannine Pitas

Calatrava's Puente de la Mujer

Buenos Aires, August 2013

I need a tango
to put things in order

please
let me touch you

even if
in the guise of another

let us lock eyes across the river
you abandoned long ago

I need to cradle
this bohemia

in parallel lines,
acute angles

I need to contain
this whirling

in the firmness
of the Puente de la Mujer

my cough, my fever
your ache, your delusion

and Calatrava's
slanted harp

all stem
from the same sweet dissonance

our story doesn't end
with a wedding

the key of our dance
will always be minor

Jeannine Pitas
Dubuque, IA

When We Were Human

When we lived in houses like books lining the shelves of Borges' library.

When each of our stories was a hagiography in the encyclopaedia of saints.

When we sat around kitchen tables sipping tea, words floating from our lips like butterflies bearing enormous scrolls.

When we unravelled that parchment and still understood the strange cursive

letters that moved and flowed like worms beneath the earth.

When we stuck our heads out the slow train's windows. Beneath us, the rails were singing.

When we got lost in a forest of conifers, when we made a wrong turn and ended up in the next town.

When we took pictures of wasps, for they too were made of light.

When we watched the rain falling gently on mushrooms.

When we stepped over wet stones in the dark forest, when we searched for stars in the mist.

When the hum of mosquitoes was still the holiest prayer.

When the veins of our hands were still roots, and flowers sprouted from them as we grew old.

Now –

Now that we know all movement is rotation.

Now that we are as motionless as stars.

Now that we search for ammonite fossils in the marble floors of shopping malls,

reaching to touch the galaxy's spiral, feeling only cracks.

Now that we neither kneel on pebbles at the river's edge nor stare down at it from high crags.

Now that we would never stop to stroke the scales of a forest snake.

Now that we don't stand up to pray the Angelus at noon, and our voices no longer touch each other like folded hands.

Now that all our languages have converged into a single word which we repeat again and again.

It is said that we have not changed.

We are told that we are as we always were.

If anything, we are greater now, closer to the angels we once prayed to.

We are told that we should be grateful, as we drift from now to now.

We are told that we are still human.

But I don't believe it.

Jeannine Pitas
Dubuque, IA

Landscape - Norman Olson

As the Road Gets Slippery

There's a storm approaching
and the road gets slippery when wet.
In these times, it's getting genuinely difficult
to be a middle of the road type of person:
the ugly gully on the political right
has an impossibly deep drop-off,
endangering everyone
on the highway we call life,
while the loose stones
all over the place
on the political left
are also distressingly threatening
since their bumpy consequences
are utterly unknowable today ...
As the road gets slippery,
we seem to be speeding up
but touching the brakes
is not an option ...

D.A. Pratt
Regina, SK CAN.

Vigas - Raindog

Education

It's a two-way mirror that has forever eluded truth
A Russian Roulette gun pointed at our youth

Children line up to be served an empty plate
Not enough rations to feed grades 2 through 8

A double barrel shot gun aimed at literacy
Biohazardous thoughts, trails of ignorance, oozing idiocy

As radioactive waves of ignorance emit over legislation
American schools don't have the tools to deliver a proper education

Poverty on the rise
Classrooms blowing up in size

As suicide becomes the norm to conform and to guide
Our children falling through the cracks try to hide what's inside

The shooter drawers near
As teachers stand with no fear

How many lives have been lost
Pencils, paper, and dreams get tossed

A Nation At Risk once again
Digital data, googled knowledge will reign

So that we can fill the pockets of the wealthy
Since we can't fund a nurse to keep our kids healthy

A vigil for the weary picket signs
As hope once again declines

Tell me again how to stop a war
Explain why education isn't worth fighting for

As peril and angst play tag on the playground
Education drops to the floor, takes cover, and holds

Holds…

Holds…

Holds till justice is found

Corine Ramirez
Pasadena, CA

Convalescent Hospital

You were in the convalescent, fourth month, the only
smiling face amongst four patients lined like bowling pins
in skinny metal beds, pinned like pins in cotton coverlets,
contained, wood visages facing swinging door that
swooshed and closed for trays, needles, pills, gauze, and
all that kept your fellows' faces glum, eyes glazed.

Yesterday you slipped from bed, landed on linoleum dust,
so now they've placed a gel pad at the edge where
slippers hit when you pull yourself upright with knuckles
curled on your walker. Now they watch like hawks, the
star of the alley now, your name in black sharpie
scrawled on caution signs pinned to your bed and walls.

You're always the star: shoulders sloped, buttocks slack,
arm drooping when you sit, glasses smudged with butter
from breakfast biscuits but who cares. Halogen examination
lamps don't out-watt your eyes. Weary fingers take your
pulse, turn you this way, that, change soiled gowns, but
can't dim the stars that illuminate your smile.

Three desiccated men lined like wood beside you, dozing,
headphones blurring snores, eyes nailed to Fox or HBO,
eyes divorced from wives, sisters, brothers who ceased
pilgrimage to these bedsides months ago. But you, you're
the star unswallowed by black holes, the star unblocked
by eclipses part or whole, starlight blooming undeterred.

Thelma T. Reyna
Altadena, CA

Toxic Masculinity

My father never taught me anything
other than how to saw women in two
with electric charisma that leaves us
both daydreaming in separate prisons
and all of them dying while waiting
for us to join them on the outside.
He taught me how to break hearts
by way of the art of self destruction.
He taught me how to rob, cheat
and steal the pants off anyone
I could manipulate. He never
taught me how to drive a car
or how to ride a bike or how to fish.
I looked in his dusty dresser drawers
for artifacts that he left behind:
his 1983 wardrobe and his last
pack of camel non filters,
half of it smoked on the day
he was captured, the other half
brittle with straws of tobacco
which tasted like a very bitter
kind of silly string that is
anything but silly
and is killing him as
he battles lung cancer
in prison. He taught me
the power of mystery
and the art of disappearing.
But it all has gone down
like a movie:
one big mushroom cloud
of devastation as we drift
further into the darkness
that my father taught me.

Kevin Ridgeway
Long beach, CA

Picnic At Rawa-Ruska
*for Father Patrick Desbois**

1.

The children are there, too.
Some know the Mozart,
Others are bored.

Late afternoon: they march around.
Imitate the soldiers.
The parents lay out the picnic.
The wursts and cabbage. The clamor for sweets.

2.

This was the verdant east,
murder fields different than the west;
The children accept it,
Keep their thoughts to themselves.
Rat-a-tat! Rat-a-tat!
They fall down brilliantly.

3.

Costly: one vital metal bullet per Jew.
Newly found, an addendum to the story.
Torn hankies wipe the milky mouths;
The real hand waves goodbye again.

Judith Robinson
Pittsburgh, PA

** Patrick Desbois is a French priest who
has newly discovered fields of bodies of Jews
murdered by the Nazis in Russia, Ukraine and
other adjacent areas.*

Poem for Poets of Crash Pads Past

pill popping poets
pot smoking poets
heroin shooting poets
coke snorting poets
crack smoking poets
poets who only smoke cigarettes
& drink coffee
poets who go to meetings
poets who work as plumbers
landlord poets
poets who farm
& give away vegetables
to hungry folks
poets who raise chickens
poets who eat what they kill
poets who play guitars
in honky-tonks
& pass the hat
poets who piss on propriety
& destroy property
poets acquainted w/ the police

poets who read Villon in jail
& can't make bail
poets who publish other poets
& collate their books by hand
poets who want to get paid
& expect everything for free
poets who pet cats
poets who kick dogs
poets who raise children
poets who abandon children
poets who beat their wives
poets who have taken their own lives
poets who are flush
poets who are down on their luck
poets who should be shot
poets who write stupid list poems
poets who send their stuff to FUCK!
poets who really need the 20 bucks

Dave Roskos
Island Heights, NJ

A Life's Dog - Steve Dalachinsky

My Odyssey, My Iliad

i.

Hubbub 'cross from posh mall,
longside railroad track sad cold facts,
a bold disheveled unlevel street Jesus
-- knotted curls, ghostly beard,
soles stigmataed by bottle shards,
bloodied but showing no pain judged 'gainst His --
preaches at pushcarts lifted from Safeway.
Remote unto self in rank raincoat,
grasping mushy cellophaned Bible,
he gestures to birds, wars with trees, feeds squirrels wafers,
seeks communion 'mid the leaves and shit,
screeches epistles at Stygian grotto rag and bone men
below chic Silicon Valley cafés
next to the center of the center where we gather near heaters
under candy cane umbrellas unsecured from patios above
to suck luke coffee, rejoice in stale tarts,
some awaiting deliverance, others the bus.

Well-suited in hole-y dissolute jeans,
parka and hiking boots, ratty mittens
and ski mask yankable like a terrorist's,
junkyard doggishly gripping black bag (needles);
I wander the asphalt with a toolbox of hope
-- rasp good cheer, sometimes schmooze,
sometimes bark advice, always offer help --
to show someone really cares;
as do other volunteers,
mostly from Stanford (Aspergians there too)
plus a few Social Register church-going elders
(laocoöns living on faith and trusts,
more into a change of spirit than a change of structure).
Doctor to no-homers, a soft-hatted healer doing his best,
I deal out crumbs, meds,
and hard-headed come-to-Jesus empty-your-pockets speeches,
calling the roll for any souls who will …

ii.

To be homeless is bad,
fretted Penelope when her man was away.
Howls in my neon head rake through rosy-fingered lenses.
One corner of a glancing-eye takes in a scowling ill lad,
thin, glazed, silent,
hanging back from the rowdy crew in the parking lot queue.
Gloomy in his spring, this boy is doomed:
tethered to oxygen, wheeling a tank,
he's ravaged, gripped to dissipate,
wither, be entombed soon
while his entrails linger,
exhumed as ugly ransom for future savage,
plundered by swift-footed groaning furies.
Polishing off today's lineup of dopers and loners,
users and losers, screamers, moaners, schemers,
smashed shoulders and dreams; as if on cue,
I make fleeting contact -- which is deflected by bronzed armor.

Marshaling a high-hearted scrap of courage,
medicine bag held firm,
I amble over uninvited,
struggle for sweet spoken words
that burst forth hot-headed,
swarms of hornets whipping my halting Spanish.
Master of the battle cry, I assault Rojelio,
"¿Cuál es su problema médico, señor?"
He removes his canula and slowly lights up
which swirls into the pea soup sky, then seethes,
"I slaved underground in Sinaloa since eleven,"
half understanding from my far-famed godlike Stanford colleagues,
"You'll die in months." Tied to the mast, sailor set to sea
without biscuit, on the street, no way home, no family or papers,
too weak to work, alone 'til the shelter reopens tonight,
strongly-greaved, unharbored, he weeps, "*Gracias*,"
in rage and despair under clumps of wild wooly Ulyssean hair.

Dr. Gerry Sarnat
Portola Valley, CA

The Girl in the Paisley Nylons

Men catch their breath
as if coming up for air
when the girl
in paisley nylons
crosses her legs
one more time.
Black patterns
on alabaster skin.

I adjust my hemline,
spot a ladder run
in my own dark hose.

That narrow line
travels down
my thigh just
when I try
sex appeal
in the Italian restaurant
where garlic recalls
Michelangelo
and pesto dreams
DaVinci.

Straw cased bottles
hang from walls
the color of Siena
and wine, that ruby nectar
turns the brain to fog,
while I watch
the run spread
ever outward
and down, down,
downward
to my ankle.

Patricia Scruggs
Chino, CA

Broken Window - Alexis Fancher

In the Soul of the Carmel River

*"The Carmel is a lovely little river. It isn't very long
but in its course it has everything a river should have."*
                                        —John Steinbeck

The crisp water tongue of the Carmel River runs northwest
through Monterey County flowing from its headwaters in
the Santa Lucia Range and the Ventana Wilderness,
slipping into the mouth of the Pacific ocean,
south of the bay of Carmel-by-the-Sea —
it's brackish water the flavor of life.

To you I have traveled along the Pacific Coast Highway
through the towering Redwoods of Big Sur beneath
its spreading hood imploring peace from the trees
and surf below, its immortal embrace swaying me,
like a monastic monk, or saint, praying for release
in sacramental silence.

Salt permeates all recollection, swollen with new rain
to overflowing —fresh and salacious, drink deeply
from these waters —influencing all surrounding
its interminable grasp; its brine and sweetness
offering asylum from all sorrow and strange
remembrance in flooding discharge.

There is a hallowed spirit here carried in these waters
sweetly wedded in time, profoundly sacrosanct in
its offering. Swallow me river —I've come to you
seeking to empty my soul and memory, immersed
in the sanctum of your stream, and merged with
the timeless rocks and words of your water.

Michael C. Seeger
Cathedral City, CA

Fast Laugh, Easy Touch

I think about the things I don't know about him,
even though we drove the California coast
from the first mission to the last
and dipped our fingers in the holy fonts
of Spanish architecture and fictions
we couldn't tell from truths.
I think about how we pretended
he'd grant the indulgence for me to buy my way
out of the knot of that tangled brown summer.
I think about the things I could have said,
the things that make me wish he'd left sooner.
I think about the things he took
or asked for without a second thought,
things that built a bottleneck of unspoken words—
sentences left out and conversations left in.
I think about the things he did say, how his long leg would hang
over the front seat of his Firebird, or how he laid me down
on his bathroom floor and covered me with soap flakes
before adding water and himself and we could never stop
seeking that again—
that fast laugh, that easy touch, our fast laugh, our easy touch,
that rumbling together.
I think about my need to rearrange
the events of his departure.
But always I see that trip to the missions.
Both of us as two dried pods in hot wind,
bumping and rattling against each other,
hoping enough agitation would force open our shells.
Always I see I'm stuck on seeing those pods
as an image I use to erase my regret of squandered time.
But I can't forget—
I can be looking in the mirror in my bedroom,
my carpool tiring of waiting
        for me,

the driver tapping the horn, and without a second thought
I no longer care who might know if I give away
what I have left of another city promise.
Looking at my reflection, the carpool driver honking,
little comradery left behind the repeated notes
     of the summons,
it's not so much the time
     that I've lost
as what I can't forget—fast laugh, fast laugh, easy touch.

Lisa Segal
Los Angeles, CA

Sunday Afternoon

A neighbor is cooking pot roast,
its aroma seeping into my apartment,
and I'm halfway to waking
from far too short of a nap.
I'm listening to Arvo Pärt
and framed in the window
hovers an inquisitive wasp.
The maple trees, nearly in fulll leaf,
dance in the light breeze,
and in the sun-filled park,
the tall West African runner,
always in red track suit,
executes his twenty laps.

The laps, leisurely and measured,
and the music, slow and elegiac,
and the diminishing flutter of leaves,
and the wasp perfectly at station,
restrain the headlong world
to the the very moment I inhabit.

Doc Sigerson
Renton, WA

Timeless

My father stares as if,
walls hold answers.
Scowling, green-tea-clouds
breathe a light rain
out his window.
Scuffed cowboy boots,
grow spider webs in the corner.
He smiles in black and white
dog-eared photographs,
cocky in naval dress.

My father's voice breaks,
as he reconstructs memories
of deafening guns,
"Boom, boom, booming" at sea.
He rattles a breath.
He can't figure out
how to get into the bathroom
with his wheelchair.

He bang, bang, bangs against
the jarred door.

He no longer smiles for cameras,
cries for no reason, pretends
to follow conversations.
My father is gone, but he left
his body behind.
I observe him,
hoping this empty shell
can answer my questions.

Questions never asked,
Why can't you say,
"I love you?'

Why can't you
hold me when I cry?

Where were you
when I needed
you?

My father and I
face each other,
strangers then,
strangers now,

strangers.

Linda Singer
Redondo Beach, CA

The Rat

Continues to haunt us
not unlike a man with a rope tail
one who left the scaffold
before given a chance to finish
what he started in the ministry
of despair in the country of fascism
in the dream listing to one side

Again the many have bought in
to a regime of Kalashnikovs
the rat sips from these guns
of the state even as it creates

a manifesto of crumbs and hungers
of biblical plagues & ringed posies
& the demise of childhood

A single bite, incisors ever
at the ready white against the void
where the appetites gather to hallucinate
where the wounded bear has no power
over the braying of the donkey
the elephant's ivories

Judith Skillman
Newcastle, WA

an old friend

he had a college degree
and a nice girl friend
I had introduced them
but he liked acid
and alcohol and porn
we all worked at the welfare office
for L.A. County and he sued them
for turning him into an alcoholic
the court appeals went on for years
and finally he got a $24,000 check
he made a copy of the check and
put it on the wall
then he cashed the check
I guess he thought that $24K
would last forever but he
spent it on acid and alcohol
one night his girlfriend came to me
because she couldn't find him she said
he was at one of those porn movie houses
on Santa Monica and Western
so we went to the Pussycat Theatre
flashed our welfare i.d. cards and
they turned the lights on for us

there were five or six guys with
jackets or popcorn on their lap
but he wasn't there turns out
he had been arrested
over at Fever Cinema
for indecent exposure earlier that night
and now he needed bail money
these stories tend to go south
as the night wears on
acid alcohol and porn
take you down some roads
and just dump you there
at 3 a.m. without a dime
this guy was a friend of mine
he finally moved out to Albuquerque
re-married his ex-wife
stopped drinking
and then killed himself
with pills in some motel

acid alcohol and porn
never is plenty
always ain't enough

Rick Smith
Alta Loma, CA

A Meditation on the Color Blue

The smithereens of a hurricane
have their dark & devastating blues,
unlike the tropical calm
of a deep turquoise blue sea.

Soothing are the blueberry,
the blue periwinkle,
the blue of a parrot,
surprise blue of an orchid.

The blues in melody
—Billie Holiday, B.B. King—
have their benefits
for voice, ear, heart.

I have seen the ice-blue
in the cleft of a glacier,
seen the steel-blue ocean
breached by a whale.

I have seen the blue city,
Chefchaoen, in the Rif Mountains
of Morocco. I've been a blue man
of the Sahara for a single day.

Give me a bright blue sky
or baby blue suede shoes
or rare blues in a rock
or a painting by van Gogh.

Give me blue and white
in flags of many nations,
the royal blue of my djellaba from Morocco,
the Blue Eye that wards off evil.

Today my private blues are packed away.
I feel only placid Pisces blues
and the blue jay squawk
does not bother me.

Clifton Snider
Long Beach, CA

Two by Donna Snyder

A downpour of yellow plums: after Rumi's The Oldest Thirst There Is

an homage to Carolyn Srygley-Moore

Somewhere outside my skull, the chirp of a bird.
At last the sound makes its way into my head.
Eyes open to dusty night. A beloved dog snores,
her head upon the pillow beside mine. Your image
appears in my hand, then a jumble of words.
A downpour of yellow plums, green alleys,
torn panties lying in the dust. Your deluge
washes away the sins of the world.

I kiss the back of my own hand,
smell the sweet scent of solace.

Donna Snyder
El Paso, TX

Accepted by Barrio Panther 2019

Dark Red

Dark red I love Lucy lips make me long
for cigarettes and sex

She stands in the shadows like a Botticelli made of marzapan
Who wouldn't want to slip sweet almond beneath the tongue?
Lips linger and intoxicate themselves beneath the pearl of an ear
Inhale the scent of flesh still warm from an indifferent sun
still moist from the exertion of making sense of the lives of men
all gone mad with sorrow

We sit and laugh at the antics of a crazy redhead goddess
The voice of an angel sings
We must not forget to breathe

Deep humid gulps of warm air swallowed
like wine drunk from a terracotta cup
a red kiss pressed against its earthy lips

Donna Snyder
El Paso, TX

Previously Published in I Am South (Virgogray Press: Austin, 2010 and 2014)

Two by t. kilgore splake

rat bastard time

old black-and-white films
wind rapidly blowing
months off calendar pages
clock's ominous ticking
hands racing around dial
earth continuously turning
nights become mornings
time quickly vanishing
nothing to be saved
nervous graybeard poet
racing toward death

t. kilgore splake
Calumet, MI

Ruin-nation - by t. kilgore splake

like dorian gray

living sheltered life
staying home with parents
reading books
watching dvd movies
playing computer games
face unlined
smooth as new infant
without distinct furrows
graybeard poet
not weathering well

features stained by life
dark cheek scar
from hockey puck shot
tough leathery skin
after seasons in outfield
taut hard textures
winters of ice fishing
tobacco and alcohol lines
deep penetrating stare
waiting morning's first drink

t. kilgore splake
Calumet, MI

MY LIFE UNDER TRUMP

Day after day
The wind blows
All the trees are stripped
No promise of shade
I can't hide

The wind sings
my ears bleed
I have only what I am

I look to the sky
I search for a dove
A white feather
Something my flesh
can believe in

I can't help myself
My heart is open
I am waiting to sing
A song of joy

Kevin Patrick Sullivan
San Luis Obispo, CA

M A N - Kit Courter

Parcel Post collage – by Patti Sullivan

IT COULD HAVE BEEN ME TOO

Near misses—that time the long-lost alcoholic uncle
crawled out from under whatever scuzzy rock he'd been
living under to make a rare family appearance
Mom laughed off his comments, his leering all in good fun
but she wouldn't let me be alone with him
Near misses—that high school boy next door
offering me lemonade when I was ten
he broke into his dad's liquor cabinet, not for booze
but for the joke glasses, drink out of them
the lady's clothes would disappear, he says drink
Walking home from school—grabbed   touched
walking home from work, walking to the store, walking
through the park, walking   walking walking
Years later, that same uncle shows up
this time at his ailing mothers house when I'm visiting
he'd aged, but do they ever grow up
I cut my stay short
there's more, of course, please
don't get me started.

Patti Sullivan
San Luis Obispo, CA

Caught in Celluloid

In this dark house the lobby mirrors are cracked,
though we're assured they're not.
Now playing: *All About Eve*,
performed with dramatic irony. A farce
where nothing is funny played without passion,
sucked out across stage and screen
minus credits. The playhouse reeks – buttered up
popcorn gone bad, stale candy spilled,
our spirits dragged down sticky aisles.

.

She began a scarecrow fashioned from star-crossed sticks,
sticking to a land of make-believe,
glitter glued to city slickers,
that need for applause, like *waves of love*
pouring over footlights, someone else's story
acted out after it's decided
we are profane, our scenes cut,
dropped from her private studio.

For a chosen few, contracts renewed
thanks to rave reviews.
There's so much to learn;
yet she never does.
Rewriting vacant plots
aimed at trusting fans who believe
those rehashed monologues.

The bumpy night:
expected;
but not the feeling
we're remnants
of a haunted theatre
trapped inside
once the doors close.

Lynn Tait
Sarnia, ONT. CAN.

Our Land Becomes

What is this where I have tumbled
What is this I have been denied
What is this my life and labor
This thing that was my heart and love
What is this where waters flowed
Now clear tubes clog and litter
What is this I looked upon   adored
This to find it eaten   destroyed
What is this my work behind me
Undone unfinished desired and waiting
What is this I tried so hard   I found
Dead in leaf belching gutters
What is this rotting beast Knowledge
This for thousands of years designed for now
Thrown upon the stony beach   my red right hand
My fingers grazed upon fish scales feeling time
Gone now my axe and wedge formed callus
Eyes cumbersome where passions once raged
What is this I walk barefoot alone unafraid
Unchallenged no pretense   home   I am Free

H. Lamar Thomas
Lawrenceville, GA

Poem in Water

By Lingering Lake
I watch a Chinese poet
with sweeping brush strokes
write characters
in water
upon the pavement.
Disciples follow in silence
under the willow trees
reading retextured liquid,
the path an impermanent context.
I can't decipher the message
of this groundling poem,
but feel unmoored
then embraced, bent and baptized,
evaporating verse
washing the dust from my heart.

Mary Langer Thompson
Apple Valley, CA

The Skylark's Lesson

Don't strive. Don't fight. Don't go
beyond yourself, tensely stretching
reaching, grasping, in an effort
to bend reality to your own will
"I want, I want, I want..."

Listen. Leave this. Relax into Love
surrounding you like the smooth surface
of a mountain lake, rosy at dawn,
reflecting clearly the splendor
of crystalline peaks, glistening
with new snow, in tranquil stillness.

Be glad, so glad. Be calm, so calm. Content.
Breathe deeply. Fill your whole being
with happiness found among white daisies,
fragrant clover and golden dandelions
on a spring meadow, under the bell
of a sky, ringing with pure tones
of a lone skylark that sings away,
up in the azure, among puffy white clouds
The sky is mirrored in the softness
of cornflowers and bluebells.

Be still, so still, like a pine forest
at noon, hot with the fullness of summer
treetops barely stirring in the light breeze
whispering to each other, to you
to the birds, weary with sleep after
the extravaganza of their dawn chorus.

"The Sun is up. The Sun is up.
The Sun is everywhere. The Sun
caresses our crowns and we
grow — grow — grow —
from deep waters of the Earth
into Sunlight."

Breathe deeply, slowly, deeply.

IN —the tension constricting your heart
with worries of today, yesterday, tomorrow.

OUT — the openness of Love, of loving all,
seeing all, touching all, being all,
flowing freely, brilliantly in waves
of liquid light—within you, around you,
over you — here, now, always, now —

Relax into Love. Be still, so still.
Be glad, so glad, content.

Blossom like the Earth's gentle smile,
like the khorovod of trees, birds' servants
sustaining all among their leaves and branches.

Is there anything you want to know?

The answer is here already,
waiting for you in the center
of your bright, open heart.

    Maja Trochimczyk
    Sunland, CA

fighting the hook

it is that time
Death has harvested some friends
and announced His claim on others
and maybe set his hook in me
I do not know
He may sit patiently on the shore
and watch me fight the hook a dozen years

while collecting others I call my friends
and others I have known
I do not know if Death has plans
or just takes what the universe deals Him
it is not my job to know
just, when the time comes,
to give him the best tail dance I can

Wyatt Underwood
Encino, CA

The Living Room - Jennifer Roskos

Where the Grapes of Wrath are Stored

See, that guy Tom Joad, in John Steinbeck's
Pulitzer Prize book Grapes of Wrath, the
author receiving a Nobel Prize, which means
what he had to say was important to many
other people, people whose opinion counts,
not just me, but better folks than me, Joad said
"…then I'll be all aroun' in the dark. I'll be
ever'where — wherever you look. Wherever
they's a fight so hungry people can eat,
I'll be there. Wherever they's a cop beatin'
up a guy, I'll be there…I'll be in the way guys
yell when they're mad an' — I'll be in the way
kids laugh when they're hungry an' they know
supper's ready. An' when our folks eat the stuff
they raise an' live in the houses they build
— why, I'll be there". I was 19 when I read
that in the living room of my yellow stucco house
in Lake Balboa CA, beneath the wood- paned
window, waiting for my working parents to arrive
from their jobs at night, right there I cast my lot
with Tom Joad, knew that to those commitments
he made, I gave my life, except I didn't have enough
of a life to give yet but I gave all I had until I could
go to War and return with a lot more to give.

Vachine
Santa Monica, CA

Dead Man 3 - Richard Vidan

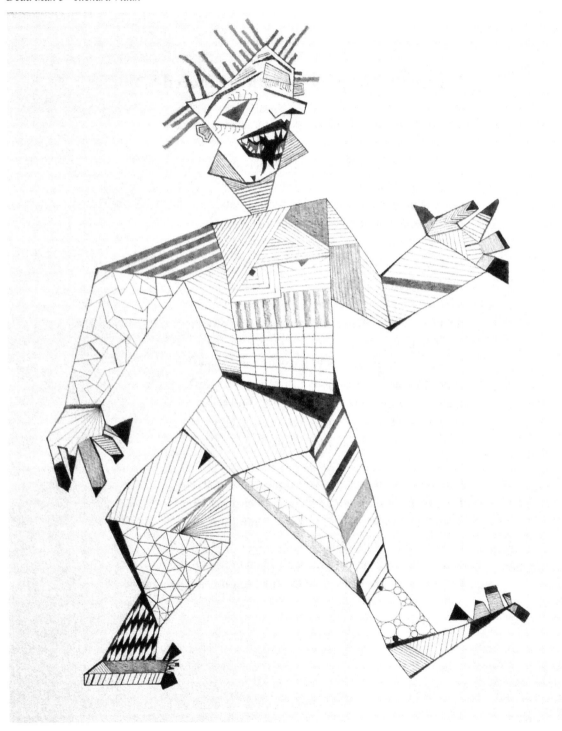

IT'S A GOOD DAY---------SO FAR

I had a not-too-terrible night's sleep
Just 2 nightmares
Nobody called at 6 am
The delivery guy put the paper on the porch
It's cold and windy but not raining
We haven't lost electricity
My feet aren't too badly numb
The furnace is still working
No trees have fallen on the house
My arthritis is only bad
I finished the crossword
I haven't stepped on a nail
Trump has yet said no more than 5 stupid things
My back hasn't gone out
My wife is driving me crazy just half the time
There have been only 7 robocalls
One time I was able to pee in less than 6 minutes
There were no bills in the mail
My gastritis didn't make me throw up after dinner
I didn't hear from any of my relatives
And my teeth aren't hurting me as much

Oh, and I haven't killed myself

Richard Vidan
Orangevale, CA

Spring is a Sign

A cross or an arrow for example;
a human with outstretched arms,
    a point, the flutter
of many wings at once.

You painted bees on your ukulele
and ran into the field;
    you dropped down
in tall grass and waited
beside the stream.

Is this the same river, is this
the same water you saw
flashing down the mountain?
    Are you the flower
you've been dreaming?

Neighbors are walking on the road,
neighbors are dying on the vine.
    We're under the continual sun
and that alone is assurance.
Beneath her chatter and laughter
the sound of soft, strong wings.

Stewart Warren
Silver City, NM

Two by Linda Whittenberg

Stone-cold

Germany, summer of 61',
they hurried to pour concrete
to build the cruel wall.
It was all the news—families split,
a bifurcated city, country.
Take Down the Wall,
was heard in streets all over
the world, until, at last,
sledgehammers did the demolition
while citizens on both sides
pocketed shards so they would
never forget.

This is a cautionary tale now that walls
are prime-time news once more.
We build them up only to be torn down,
or they crack, mortar crumbles.
More often, no one lives who

remembers why they were built at all.
Even walls inside ourselves
want to be dismantled stone by stone
or even smashed in a fit of triumph.
When what we were protesting
no longer needs that wall,
many Hallelujahs are in order,
celebrate! Take a memento,
put it in a poem.

Linda Whittenberg
Santa Fe, NM

Weather Report

Today the weather is George Winston
as I first heard him coming in
over ceiling speakers at the gift shop
at Big Sur on a day overcast with wind
that worked its way through winter coats
and has stirred up choppy waves.

It's a stay-home-from-the-gym day,
an improvised comfort-music kind of day,
nothing to stir up a storm like Coltrane or
Miles, not even as dramatic as Keith Jarret
or with the inventive energy of Winton,
definitely not edgy or electronic.

It's late April, but winter can't quite
let go. We've had ragged jazz for weeks,
the kind gifted musicians play only
for each other, freezing the apricot buds,
sweet pink blossoms of peach.
I'm ready for Firebird,

Stravinsky, Tchaikovsky, Shostakovich
the Russians know how to stir the blood.
They were my first love, an LP
of Rachmaninoff's Concerto No. 2
in C# Minor when I was sixteen
and first notes of lust were stirring.

I wore the grooves down on that LP,
playing it while I did homework,
waiting for life to begin, the way it is, also,
when you feel there's not much living left
and you're impatient spring to come
I've always thought George Winston
monotonous.

Linda Whittenberg
Santa Fe, NM

Unalome as a Tattoo

Under a moon surely full,
one final healing
at the conjunction
of an open chakra chalice
and an overflowing heart.
Preparations, deep in the embrace
of the Saguaros of Sabino Canyon.
This latest fool's path
strewn both with Spring blossoms
and their accompanying thorns.
The sternum leads in procession.

Surer now of power held,
of certainty earned.
The Church Ink priestess, Marcella,
here to dialogue with
my stubborn insistence.
Simplifying this journey
still more
in disallowing time.
My own warrior gifts me
with the larger questions.
Tools for this initiation.

Pamela Williams
Silver City, NM

Slash Cutting - Raindog

MICRO-FICTION

FEAR MOVES TO A NEW TOWN

MANX SAT across from the La Salle, enjoying his coffee as he opened his mail. The morning sun was doing its best to cut through the chill of early winter. It was not very successful. Every so often, someone (probably some drunk) would let out a scream from across the street. It was natural. Life is a truly scary proposition these days, and the shock of living it would make the most sane among us cry out if we hadn't been conditioned since birth to do otherwise. As he contemplated this (and the swirls in his cappuccino) a youth, of passing acquaintance, sat down (uninvited) at the table and began to rant.

"Truth is a broken mirror. Justice is an empty box. Intimacy is a suicide note. Desire is an empty shot glass."

Your point being...? Manx thought.

Was this really news to the kid? The world was neither safe nor sanitized; yet every time you turned on the box there was some government stooge trying to convince you otherwise. Likewise, every time you went out there was some goon preaching righteous indignation from a makeshift pulpit. Or some kid who had just discovered that life sucked, preaching to the choir at some poetry 'reading' or in some alley where the 'chronic' burned and spoiled dreams mingled with spilt booze. He wondered where these people had been? How had they missed the decline and fall of practically everything sacred?

The kid was on a roll now. He knew it and Manx knew it. Trouble was, he wanted nothing to do with the kid. The kid brought out a fear that had plagued him for years. A fear which he had learned to suppress by ignoring it. A fear that had gone unnamed for years: homophobic. Not as in homosexual fear, but as in homo-sapien fear.

He looked at the kid. He wished he could make the kid disappear... forever. He wondered what would happen? Could he get away with it? Would anyone notice? According to the kid, no one gave a damn if he was ever heard from again. Manx drifted into a murderous daydream of doing vile things to the kid (just to show him how bad it could really get) before dropping him head-first down a mineshaft out in the Panamints, or maybe, over by Pinto Basin*.

"Truth is a handful of dirt. Justice is the open grave."

A scream punctuated this statement. Manx lurched forwards out of his chair, his letters scattering like bystanders at a drive-by shooting. His hands clutched the kid's throat. It was soft and innocent like a Harp seal. He choked out the words as Manx brought down the club.

"Beauty is getting what you wished for... whether you like it or not."

"Too true, too true;" thought Manx.

He was long over-due for a change of scenery, anyway.

RD Armstrong
Long Beach, CA

Pinto Basin has a bad reputation: a place of bad medicine and the black (he)arts. Located northeast of Josha Tree National Park, in California.

THE SHAMAN

THE SHAMAN climbed the mountain, gathered sacred flowering herbs and berries along the way -- Datura moonflowers, toloache, Brugmansia angel's-trumpets, Salvia apiana sage, kasiile, toyon, holly -- until delirium overwhelmed him with lurid and ecstatic visions of hell and heaven. Then he returned to the human world.

Word spread of him. People asked, "Is it true, as they say, that you have seen hell?" "I have." "What's it like?" "It's hideous, ironic, horror beyond imagination," the shaman winced as he relived it, nearly blinded by his recollection: "There's food everywhere, but no one eats, and drink aplenty, but no one drinks. There are long wooden spoons with which to partake, but their bodies have only tiny appendages for arms, too short to bring such elongated spoons up to their shriveled lips. Parched slaver forms like ashes in their mouths. Their bodies waste away. Struggle as they might, everything goes to ruin. They bellow in agony." The people shrank away, with growing acreage dedicated to burying their discarded surplus collapsing under smoldering heaps of waste.

"And heaven?" asked the hopeful. "Is it true, as they say, that you have seen heaven?"

"I have." "And what's it like?" they pleaded. "Heaven," the shaman revealed, "heaven is exactly the same."

"What," cried the people, "the same? Surely that is no heaven!" "There is one difference," the shaman went on to explain. "In heaven, there is a stunning abundance of food and drink, long wooden spoons with which to partale, and bodies with tiny appendages instead of arms too short to bring these long utensils up to their mouths. But the beings there, without hesitation, use the long wooden spoons to feed one another. There is no want. No request goes unanswered, no desire unfulfilled. Acts of kindness overflow as do the spoons. Spoon fed and cared for, there are continuous cries of celebration, gratitude, and rejoicing as the contented beings fall over one another to be the first to give. There is food, and they eat. There is drink, and they drink, and they relish a bounty of diversity. They care for one another, nourish one another, thank one another. The gentleness of their words and kindness of their eyes..." the shaman wept. "I only wish I could have shown one world to the other."

Seven Dhar
Altadena, CA

LIVES CHANGE

ONE AFTER another, weary footsteps brought him closer; until he could see in the distance the welcoming haven he called home. It had been his home for many winters – longer than any other he had in his life. Each move had been necessary because another came along who could do his job better.

There was comfort in the familiar landmarks he had gotten used to; the huge elm tree to his left; the row of elders opposite and the prickly shrubs outside his entrance that flowered each spring.

He felt a lump in his throat at the injustice of his lot. I'm not really old, he thought, and the time passed so quickly…too quickly.

It seems just yesterday I was in my prime, on top of the world where nothing could touch me. Today I'm a has been, getting just enough to see me through---when I get anything at all.

Each day he had to wear longer and harder. A stronger rival had appropriated his territory and since then, his loss of prestige threatened his existence.

Safely inside he relaxed his tense body and snuggled down into the warm bed. One more day, he thought, but how long it will last, I don't know.

There's always another who is bigger, stronger, and more cunning just waiting to make a move and take over all I've worked so hard to get.

He knew he had to move and wondered how he had managed to stay here as long as he did. Already there were rumblings because he was envied the choice location of his home.

His successor, he knew, would make a move soon and there would be no way to stop the chain of events. His one-time companions now shunned him, preferring to be associated with a winner hoping some of the bounty would come their way. Even his mate had left him, wanting a younger more aggressive male.

The twilight sounds were familiar to him; so familiar that he could pick up and react to a foreign sound—as he did now. They were gathered outside, he knew, not waiting any longer to evict him. He wished he could just slink off into oblivion but knew he had to put up some sort of protest, even a token one. He knew the terror that had to be on his face. He'd seen it hundreds of times before on the faces of his own victims as he had built his own empire in the days of his youth.

Outside he approached them with slow prodding steps, head held high in a last effort of bravado. They were all there. Some had brought their families to witness the humiliation. He looked into the eyes of his former comrades seeing nothing but pleasure at his come-down. He envied them for a moment. They had conformed early in life and their positions were secure.

Once he had branded them coward and sneered at them for accepting les. Yes, maybe he deserved all this, but, still, it was all so unfair. At the last moment he looked up. To see the cruel eyes and the sharp teeth of the largest gray wolf. The new leader of the pack.

Helen Donahoe
Pittsburgh, PA

She Says Stalker/He Says Fan

"If you can't be free, be a mystery." - Rita Dove, 'Canary.'

SHE'S A singed torch song, a broken chord, the slip-shadow between superstar and the door. She's that long stretch of longing riding shotgun from nowhere to L.A., a bottle of Jack Daniels snug between her thighs, always some fresh loser at the wheel. She's the Zippo in your darkness, a glimmer of goddess in your god-forsaken life, her voice a rasp, a whisky-tinged caress. She *gets* you, and you know the words to all her songs, follow her from dive bar to third-rate club clapping too loudly, making sure she makes it home. She's as luckless in love as you are, star-crossed, the pair of you, (in your dreams). If only we could choose who we love! Tonight the bartender pours your obsession one on the house, dims the lights in the half-empty room as she walks on stage, defenseless, but for that 0018 rosewood Martin she cradles in her lap like a child. If you ask nicely, she'll end with the song you request night after night, about the perils of unrequited love. You'll blurt out your worship into her deaf ear, while her fingers strum your forearm and her nails break your skin. *Give the lady whatever she wants*, you'll tell the barkeep. Like that's even possible.

Alexis Rhone Fancher
San Pedro, CA

_____

First published in The San Pedro River Review "Music" Issue. 2018

For Sarah

JACK STOOD at the corner of Hollywood and Vine having coffee with his ex. But this was not the usual kind of coffee visit. As he poured a stream of liquid dark roast onto the pavement and watched it roll into the curbside grating, a beautiful wispy steam appeared. He loved this. What he thought of as the energy of Sarah. And it made him happy every day for a month now that any drunken idiot could murder the body of a person, but no one can kill the energy of human spirit

Roseanna Frechette
Denver, CO

PAPOULIS

AFTER COMPLETING his BA in history at UCSB, and a teaching credential, George Papoulis began to believe that he was the son of God. Then he became convinced that a secret Nazi cabal was out to get him, due to his Greek roots. After a shouting match with his family, men in white coats wrestled him into a straight-jacket, and he was carted off to a state facility for seven weeks.

With a new lease on life, via daily doses of powerful anti-psychotics and mood elevators, he began teaching at Locke High in South LA. It was stressful job, with high levels of class-room chaos.

After a particularly bad week, he decided to cut loose at the Red Onion disco in Redondo Beach. During the '70s, this was a notorious party spot.

George set an intention to find a woman. He approached the crowded bar, and drank one Cadillac Margarita after another, until he lost count. With an explosive head of sugar and alcohol, he walked up to a woman with a teased-up beehive hairdo and a voluptuous figure.

"Hey, wanna dance?" he asked.

She glanced up at him. "Yeah, Ok."

George didn't really know how to dance. But the alcohol made that irrelevant. After gyrating wildly through one song, they went back to the bar.

"My name is Charlene," she said.

"I'm George. Hard to hear. So loud!"

"I know!" Charlene replied.

"Do you want to go somewhere?" George asked.

She paused. "Well, we could go to my place."

"Where is that?"

"Downey," she replied.

"Downey! I don't even know where that is. It sounds far."

"It's not that far at night. The traffic is light."

"I'm part Greek. Is that Ok?"

"Sure. I'm part Mexican. Who cares?"

George felt relieved.

"I'm with a friend. I'll go tell her that I'm leaving," she said.

After what seemed an interminable drive, from freeway-to-freeway in George's 1964 VW Beetle, they arrived at a tiny stucco house with a chain link fence around the front yard.

As soon as they were inside the front door, they began ravenously making out, then she led him to a side bedroom where they tore each other's clothes off and made frantic love.

When it was over, they both lay in the twisted covers heaving for breath. Then George was out. He was quite drunk.

When he awoke, it was pitch black. He squinted at the tiny glowing markers on the hands of his watch. About 4:05.

He unsteadily got out of bed and started looking for his clothes. When he was almost dressed, she awoke. She jumped out of bed in the nude, and turned on the light.

"Are you trying to sneak out?!"

"Umm, I need to go. I'm a long way from home."

"We need to go see a priest! I think I love you!"

"I hardly know you. I don't even know your last name!"

"I need some help from a man. A good man."

"This is too much. I'm a new teacher. And I'm a schizophrenic."

"And I have three children! This is my father's house. We live with him. He took the kids overnight to Disneyland, so I could have a little break."

She began to cry. Running mascara. "I just needed a little break."

They both stood in silence, bathed in the harsh glare of the overhead light. Then George approached her and kissed her on the lips.

"You are a beautiful woman," he said. "Any man would be lucky to have you. But I'm tread-ing water as fast as I can, just to keep my head above the waves."

"So am I," she said.

"I have to go," he said, as he headed toward the door.

On the way home, as the sun was coming up, he cried.

Michael Meloan
Los Angeles, CA

THE LANGUAGE OF CORN

Art that has endured has a quality we call schmaltz or corn.
        Richard Hugo

CORN ALWAYS wanted popularity, so the more variety, the better. You can have Strawberry for poppability, the Baby (creamy for salads and Asian cuisine), the old Shoe-peg, the Tri-color (said to be resistant to malaria), and the Silver Princess— white and "oh-so-sweet." Other varieties include Hog corn and the Country Gentleman. Most blasphemous are folks who use plastic holders. What a sumptuous experience to waste, cradling the huge, dripping cylinder, the firmer the grip, the easier bite. It's all yours, the deep scoop, empty sockets to play with, tonguing. Corn likes chemicals. Side dressing of nitrogen steps up profits. Corn likes parties, wants its own masquerade, its own show, own costume, its own get-up, say a cloak that transforms into a puppet (*Korn-popel*).

The woman who shucks the last cob is lucky enough to get the "Old Man." She is dressed in pease-straw and carried to the barn. All the harvesters dance her around until the straw falls off. A real hoedown! She knows the younger threshers are nude under their overalls. In spirit, the "Old Man" is banished to outbuildings for the winter. After the last harvest, the Corn-cock roams the fields waiting to peck the eyes of dawdling children. Some nail a live cock to the barn door as a warning and leave him until the last snow melts. If the farmer's wife cannot find a real stubble-cock for the harvest meal, she resorts to Cock-a-Leekie, a soup make from fowl broth and leeks.

There may be many puppets in the barn this winter.

Jeanine Stevens
Sacramento, CA

*Harvest examples inspired by The Golden Bough: A Study of Magic and Religion,
-Sir James Frazer.*

A Red Mule Named Red Mule

SUDDEN WINDSTORMS breaking down on the mountains into cornfields and cow pastures, where no stallions run, no Westerns linger, no mares, no geldings, just a lone red mule gazing a mule gaze into the woods where ghost mists rise after dusk and he finds a friend. China Gate chimes singing beyond harmony, somewhere into "Music for 18 Musicians", oak and pine walls groan pushing back against the fat rains of April playing games with the seasons, and the front porch stayed steady; yet, cherry tomatoes lost today as the giant, shining, green glazed Georgia clay pottery was blown leaf like along the rails, hard upon the river stone path, it shattered as if it were cheap crystal. All things die and everything solid melts. Not depressing, just the story of life.

Broke down, busted, drained of ambition I stood and watched Winter work destroyed. As the low storm cloud dark day turned to waxing moonlight, it seems another world walked in and promised something different would arise, so be still and pay attention to the strange constellations deep beyond the ring around the moon. Watch things change. I did. There are other sprouts waiting in trays in the near shed, no worry now. Right? Musk, the smell of musk is everywhere, a white truffle smell, the hollow was a basement. Rotting leaves turn to ferns, and new rows of corn, long beans and purple tomatoes grow. Horses and cows warily pace themselves out of the barns and see the fields of buckwheat and clover are doing well and ready to be there for them to graze and laze upon.

Yeah, the living ain't easy and there is never a promise of friendship, a better tomorrow, whatever that is, like it's a cup of dreams hanging on waiting for This reality to begin. It never begins. It just is. Take this attention span and make murals of wishes on hillsides. I have no use of them anymore, all I want? to live and work the land with my red mule. Playing out verses of the melancholy Dane in E# major on a well-tuned studio Yamaha, notes sustained and gripping the windows to give a shake to the day before my thoughts run astray of staying on the road between suffering and overcoming, well, I wish. Why not dream?

There's my sweet white Boxer who calls herself Daisy and is always nearby guarding me from mystery, waiting to be groomed, and fed, with each bowl a glory of happiness, she dances around and gobbles down, I laugh and say "Mercy!" you made me smile. My own dinner is a fixation, a mass of colors laying out on the counter, call it a bounty. Hot pecan oil, steel wok bringing blazing heat for quickly cooked leaves and vegetables. I eat the season, we eat the season, we stop the separation from time to eat as earth says. I do not want anything more of the ways of life today, push the vampire hearts away… Take them away! I blink. Oh, there is an order to things around here, certainly not there in all of the citylands, your smothering suburbs, burning asphalt and temperatures rising higher by the hour. I walk away in the treeline towards a trail up this mountain. Sit awhile Peace. Each tree, each animal, each bird and even white pines have a brighter story. Give me their fables over hell world voted in by idiot masses and drunken crones. Meditation. There is peace in simply being here. What about out there? Well out there New America is burning, and I want nothing of its lies and tragedy. See ya at dinner! Clanging triangles and singing bowls, calling to the fields again, It's time for dinner! Remember fresh, spring water, eating vegetables on the land they were grown? Ask the red mule named Red Mule just how good pale corn ground to grits can really be.

H. Lamar Thomas
Lawrenceville, GA

You can call me Mom

You can call me Mom. That's what she said to me 25 years ago; the woman with a rosary winding around the left side of her heart and a wooden cross with Jesus holding up the mechanical valve on the right...beat beat...beat beat. That's what this Catholic woman with cropped hair the color of a sandstorm and oversized round glasses said to the Jewish woman creating a family with her daughter; You can call me Mom.

On my 54th birthday, I listened to the rosary said again and again while her 27 x 42 picture glared at me as I sat in a Catholic Church situated on a dusty road in Santa Fe. It didn't feel like a day to celebrate.

As I heard her best friend of 60-something years explain how she was like a sister, it didn't feel like a day to celebrate. As I listened to a 20 person choir harmonize to 10 guitarists playing a mariachi-inspired hymn, it didn't feel like a day to celebrate. As I watched my son cradle my daughter while tears cascaded down his cheeks, it didn't feel like a day to celebrate. As I squeezed my partner's hand knowing that the hole in her heart was more massive than the Grand Canyon, it didn't feel like a day to celebrate.

Last year on my 53rd, she left a voicemail singing "Happy Birthday to you..." just like every year since 1992. This year, I sat on a wooden pew. It didn't feel like a day to celebrate.

You can call me Mom. That's what she said to me 25 years ago.

Felice Zoota-Lucero
Los Angeles, CA

ARTICLES

THOUGHTS ON THE WHITMAN BICENTENIAL + 2 POEMS

Walt Whitman Ekphrastic

I never look at it. I always skip past
the woodcut portrait in Leaves of Grass.

I think it's a woodcut, but I can't say.
I'm typing into a blank laptop screen.
Nor do I know what edition. Or what year.
I think he's got a hat on and his arms are crossed.
He may also be balding. I'm not sure.
Maybe a funky belt hangs loose around
his middle aged waist. And out there on the

edges I imagine there are small ink dots,
sort of fading around the lines. I don't know

if there are wrinkles around his eyes. And
even if there were, I think they'd only be

suggested. Maybe his arms are open wide,
hat in hand, standing like my grandfather

who worked a linotype machine in lower
Manhattan. I wish I could show you both
this device I'm working on. The way

it answers all these questions, but I'm not
going to Google. Instead, I imagine you posing

and now someone is asking you to hold still
and you, Walt Whitman, are looking at us.

Henry Crawford
Silver Spring, MD

---

*First Published in Mannequin Haus, Issue 11
Published in the Walt Whitman 200 Anthology,
Endlessly Rocking, May 2019*

WALT WHITMAN: RADICAL OPTIMIST?

by RD Armstrong

SOME BRIGHT young scholar at UCLA put forth the idea that Walt Whitman was a Radical Optimist (whatever that means) and this was snapped up by academia for this year, the **200th anniversary** of his birth. A milestone to be sure, but what does it mean? I suppose it depends on which lenses one chooses to look through. If we look at his avocations and employment history, we see a brilliant mind embracing a particularly "American", i.e., nationalist reference point of view; but on the otherhand, he was certainly radical in his beliefs (that everyone, regardless of societal labels, should be treated with respect). In this I'd say Whitman was certainly an Idealist.

But who was this man, who later became known affectionately as the *Good Gray Poet* (coined by William Douglas O'Connor) or *Uncle Walt* (to the troops he cared for during the Civil War)?

Whitman was born in 1819 in Long Island, NY, into a country that wasn't even 50 years old. He was the second of nine children, living in a small house (on a corner lot of the family's ancestoral estate, which had been settled in the 1640s). When he was 8, Long Island abolished slavery. This was 36 years before President Lincoln delivered the Emancipation Proclamation abolishing slavery in all of America. You could say that Whitman was born into slavery or the idea that certain members of society were less than human (an idea that still has roots in this country). Unlike the prevailing beliefs of his generation, Whitman freed himself from the tyranny of slavery, describing himself as "an American, one of the roughs, a kosmos, disorderly, fleshly, and sensual, no sentimentalist, no stander above men or women or apart from them, no more modest than immodest" (Wikipedia, Early Career [54]).

At the age of 11, Walt left home and went to work; his many jobs included pressboy, typesetter, clerking for a lawyer, gofer, Op-ed editor and roving reporter. By the age of 21, he was operating a weekly newspaper on his own. He was the publisher, editor, typesetter, printer, distributor, and news "boy" (kinda like LUMMOX Press's Raindog). Clearly he was developing the skills needed to self-publish the book for which he is best known, *Leaves of Grass*; as well as developing a better understanding of the world at large. At one point he even worked for newspaperman Samuel Clemens (Mark Twain). He wrote several books and tracts but was most noted for Leaves of Grass, which he began working on in 1850 when he was 36 years old.

At first, Leaves of Grass (first published in 1855) was lauded for it's use of plain spoken and honest language (poetry to this point was written in the "English" style with rhymeschemes and stilted language.... it was clearly not meant for the people as a whole). Whitman changed all that. His poetry flowed, weaving in and out of dialect, exploring ideas hitherto considered disreputeable and, in some cases, pornographic! His epic poem, *Song of Myself*, which took up most of the first version of Leaves of Grass, did explore sexuality in most of its forms, certainly homosexuality, which is still abhorent in our 'enlightened' world, some 128 years after his death! Because of this phobia, Leaves of Grass was tainted in the minds of some and this would continue to be the case for the rest of his life.

A year before the beginning of the Civil

Walt Whitman at 50 - by unknown

War (1861 - 1865), Whitman's first printing of Leaves of Grass had been out for 5 years. It had done well, selling out the run of nearly 800 copies; then in 1860 a second volume was published and later a third, more-expanded version in 1867. Each successive volume was re-edited, refined and the ideas he deemed important, rehoned. When the final version was published in 1889, he wrote, "L. of G. *at last complete*—after 33 y'rs of hackling at it, all times & moods of my life, fair weather & foul, all parts of the land, and peace & war, young & old."

In the beginning of the war, amidst the hoopla and patriotic displays, Whitman (even though he was raised as a Quaker) wrote a poem entitled *Beat! Beat! Drums!* which served as a ralleying cry for Union forces going into battle (with the assumption that the superiority of the Union would crush the Confederacy and break their will to fight, in just a few weeks). Sadly, this was not the case. A trip to the front lines brought the horrible waste of life to him when he all but fell into a huge pile of severed limbs. This stirred Uncle Walt (who was humanist, a transcendentalist, and pacifist) to volunteer as a nurse in Army hospitals for those wounded and maimed in battle (be they Union or Confederate soldiers). The war and the assassination of President Lincoln had a profound effect on him. His poem O Captain, My Captain moved

---

SOME EVENTS YOU MIGHT FIND OF INTEREST:

Now until Jan. 1, 2020
UCLA is conducting several programs dealing with "Uncle Walt". Contact the English Dept. for more information.

May 30 - December 7
Rutgers-Camden Center for the Arts
-Stedman Gallery
314 Linden Street
Camden, New Jersey 08102

August 31 - November 30
Camden County Historical Society
1900 Park Blvd.
Camden, NJ 08103

October 3 - December 14
Center for Book Arts
28 West 27th Street, 3rd Floor
New York, NY 10001

October 15 - January 5, 2020
Providence Athenaeum
https://providenceathenaeum.org/

---

the nation and (if possible) helped heal this fractured land.

One of the certainties of Whitman's place in American literary achievement is that his seminal work, self-published in 1855 "Leaves of Grass", was in free verse form and contained subject matter that challenged poetic and societal conventions of the 19th century. The poet and essayist Ralph Waldo Emerson wrote of Whitman after receiving the poems (L of G) that it was "the most extraordinary piece of wit and wisdom" America had yet contributed. Whitman's poetic voice spoke in an ideal, inclusive democratic persona that projected an equality that then - just as today – did not exist. He commiserated with the plight of laborers which naturally would extend to those in servitude. He frequently wrote in the voice of the *oppressed*.

Whitman who dedicated his craft to praising the natural state of men and women of all ages and races in language that was accessible and plain spoken. He sought to invent an entirely fresh—and singularly American—poetic, whose subject matter was centered on the everyday circumstances of life and the lives of common people. Perhaps the *Good Gray Poet* was actually a radical idealist!

Leaves of Grass, 1855 – 1891, featured a number of long poems including: "Hush'd Be the Camps To-Day" (1865); "I Sing the Body Electric" (1865); "O Captain! My Captain!" (1865); "One's Self I Sing" (1867); "Pioneers! O Pioneers!" (1865); "Song of Myself" (1855); "Song of the Open Road" (1856);

"This Dust Was Once the Man" (1871); "When Lilacs Last in the Dooryard Bloom'd" (1865).

For more on Walt Whitman's life go to Wikipedia.

I conclude with this poem (by Gil Hagen Hill) as further proof that Walt Whitman still lives in the hearts of many poets...

We Was Robbed...

Walt you old queer bastard
You sang of the coming
Of democracy to the republic- you believed -
As I once believed.

Doomed by money lenders
And other frauds, we worked
Their land, we built their
Babylon, everybody has a price.

Empty factories, rail car after
Rail car pass, the asphalt heats
Up a baffled kingdom a black
Sun. Walt you old queer bastard

We was robbed...we was lied
To...war and peace somewhere,
Everywhere in between...we overthrew the
Status quo and built new ones

More things more people... justice
Mercy, equality - just words no
Meat no potatoes! Walt those
Young boys you saw through

Tent flap what'd they die for a
More perfect union? The Emancipation
Proclamation , manifest destiny,
God and country, there is no god.

Walt it's a freak show! Minute by
Minute blow by blow ... the heart and mind
Beaten. Walt you old queer bastard
Ain't what you saw was amputated

Arms and legs foot to hand
Elbows akimbo ankle to heels
Heads to chest flesh to frame

An endless file of corpses....

Gil Hagen Hill

POETRY X HUNGER: LOOKING INTO THE EMPTY CUPBOARD

by Hiram Larew

For this lovely bowl
Let us arrange some flowers
Since we have no rice

Matsuo Basho (b. 1644 – d. 1694)

FOR AS long as hunger, famine and starvation have plighted the planet, there surely have been poets writing about the scourge. The master haikuist, Basho, offered his bittersweet take nearly four centuries ago. Other poets have written about hunger in Contemporary and Colonial America, Africa, Europe and throughout Asia – wherever hunger has haunted.

In large measure, however, the voice of poets against hunger has been and continues to be muted. Although taken up by science and other professional communities including some in the arts, hunger has yet to be as fully, widely and deeply described and decried by the poetry community. While poverty, homelessness, illness and social inequities continue to be popular subjects of moving and rousing poetry, for whatever reasons, the inventory of poetry focused on hunger is relatively meager and uncurated. This note describes a proactive effort – borne of my interest in both poetry and hunger -- to engage poets in the U.S. and overseas, including young people, in lending their collective voices to confronting food insecurity and hunger.

Poetry X Hunger, an informal initiative begun in 2018, is designed to uncover and showcase both historical and contemporary hunger-focused poetry and to encourage today's poets to write about the personal, social, and political causes and impacts of hunger – all with the intent of bringing poetry more fully and intentionally to bear in our efforts to prevent and eliminate hunger in the U.S. and around the world. Placing such poems more squarely in public venues – as meeting openers, on website banners, in classrooms discussions – is a key step in *Poetry X Hunger*'s cause.

The statistics are daunting: About 15% of Americans today -- 18 million households – are food insecure and one in five college students in the U.S. are similarly threatened by hunger. Across the globe, about one billion mothers, fathers, kids and elders do not have access to sufficient or good quality food; they are starving, malnourished, stunted or chronically hungry. Hunger is also tragically paradoxical in its occurrence; many of those who are at most risk are small holder farmers, i.e. food producers in developing countries. Also, as it ravages, it does so in the face of worldwide spikes in obesity due to poor food quality and life styles. And food is wasted – as much as 40 % is thrown out in the U.S. alone, and even higher levels of food rot and spoilage are seen in many other countries.

What role can poetry play in the face of such harrowing facts? How can poetry help? The overall premise of *Poetry X Hunger* is that in the ongoing and difficult fight against hunger, the power of poetry to move hearts and minds must be energized. In so many ways, poetry can speak on key wavelengths that statistics, policies and other forms of calls-to-action simply can't. Said slightly differently…In the "let's use all tools in the toolkit" mode, shouldn't we be fully tapping into poetry's potential?

One way that *Poetry X Hunger* is prompting such poetry is to highlight stark accounts of starvation from centuries ago. While not poems, per se, these testimonies are terribly evocative and may move today's poets to compose.

For example, here's a stark account of starvation from Colonial Jamestown, VA 1623/24

…and that in the depth of winter, when by reason of the cold it was not possible for us to endure to wade in the water (as form[er]ly) to gather oysters, to sattisfie our hungrie Stomaks; but constrained us to digg in the ground for unholsom rootes … so that famine compeld us wholely to devo[u]r those hoggs, doggs, and horses that were then in the Colony, together w[i]th what rates, mice, snakes, or what vermine or Carion soever we could light one… [From the Virginia Company Archives]

And the following tragic letter, written during the Great Ukrainian/Russian Famine of 1932/33, is quoted in Robert Conquest's 1986 book, *The Harvest of Sorrow*, published by Oxford University Press.

MY BELOVED SON,
This is to let you know that your mother is dead. She died from starvation after months of pain. I, too, am on the way, like many others in our town. There is [no food] for hundreds of miles around here. Your mother's last wish was that you, our only son, say Kadish for her. Like your mother I, too, hope and pray that you may forget your atheism now when the godless have brought down heaven's wrath on Russia. Would it be too much to hope for a letter from you, telling me that you have said Kadish for your mother – at least once – and that you will do the same for me? That would make it so much easier to die. [Original source: W. I. Reswick, I Dreamt Revolution, Chicago, 1952, pp. 308-309.]

In addition to providing historical context, *Poetry X Hunger* provides other incentives to write hunger-focused poetry. In partnership with the United Nations' Food and Agriculture Organization, the initiative offered a 2018 World Food Day (October 16) Poetry Competition to poets in suburban Maryland, Virginia and Washington, DC. First Place ($1000) Winner, Aaron R. of Arlington, VA presented his poem, *Hunger Pains*, in October, 2018 to a standing room only crowd of hunger specialists and poets, and he is scheduled to offer it at upcoming meetings of agricultural development experts. His poem as well as many others that were submitted are posted on Facebook at *Poetry X Hunger -- https://www.facebook.com/Poetry-X-Hunger-1874313762632994/*

And, the Maryland State Arts Council recently awarded a Creativity Grant to *Poetry X Hunger* for building and extending the initiative's web and social media platforms as places where more poems by Maryland-based and other poets can be presented and discussed.

To be clear, *Poetry X Hunger* 's work will not end hunger. Its more modest intent is to enlist the voices of poets from Basho forward in the ongoing struggle against hunger. In so doing, *Poetry X Hunger* will hopefully rouse, shame and energize public hearts and consciences in ways that amplify political- or science-based calls-to-action. This, all for the sake of our 18 million American families and the 11 billion people worldwide who are hungry.

For more info, *PoetryXHunger@gmail.com* or *HLarew@gmail.com*.

Hiram Larew, April 2019

TONY SCIBELLA: THE POET IN AMERICA

by John Macker

> *"O ocean*
> *gull*
> *poem & voice*
> *adieu & adios*
> *venice*
> *pals: i*
> *hope that that will do it."*

TONY SCIBELLA, an artist and poet, (1933-2003) was one of the founders, along with poets Stuart Z. Perkoff, Frank T. Rios, John Thomas, Philomene Long, novelist Alexander Trocchi, and others, of the Venice West literary arts scene south of Los Angeles beginning in the 1950's. This was the genesis of the So-Cal Beat counter-culture in American letters, a short 380 miles south of Haight-Asbury.

Novelist/hipster/mentor Lawrence Lipton did his best to spotlight the Venice art scene with his ridiculous memoir, *The Holy Barbarians*, which did much accidentally to satirize the fairly serious culture of poets and painters for the tourists, who then flocked to Venice Beach in invasive pastel droves, looking for the beatniks. As Hillary Kaye put it in the *Free Venice Beachhead*, "It was a different Venice then. It was a breathing space between real estate booms. No bike path, no skate rentals, no sunglass vendors, no upscale restaurants, no valet service, no Hollywood celebrities, no gentrification, no ego sized mansions lining the canals. Venice was as simple as a Taoist dream. It was sufficiently primitive enough to pass for a seedy border town for Orson Welles' classic film 'Touch of Evil."

As Tony himself wrote in his epic poem/autobiography *The Kid in America* (Denver: Passion Press, 2000) "...Venice was a summertown the locals rented rooms to vacationers from the city & then it closed in winter showed some snowcone life on weekends& drowsed u cd rent a whole house for 65$ ...the people flee the city for the burbs forgetting the entire beach (bless em) a cheap pursuit of craft a place to do it described as a slum I never saw it thus: it is a bleedin paradise I reckoned salts on the sun oceanmotion gullquiet beach"

By 1960, outlaw bikers, drugs, sadistic beat cops and bad press put the brakes on this lively movement before it could gain any legitimate international traction. By then, the "San Francisco Renaissance" was attracting much of the mainstream media and featured a tested and savvy clique of literary gurus who had been battle-hardened by intense press scrutiny and such spectacles as the *Howl* obscenity trial and the soon-to-be-legendary Six Gallery reading.

Unnerved and enervated, by the early 1960's, many of the writers and artists left the area and scattered across America in order to pursue their careers in relative peace. A few didn't survive the psychic and physical onslaught of addiction, poverty and jail.

Tony continued making collage, writing and publishing his poetry and that of his friends. He helped poet William J. Margolis put out the literary magazine, *Miscellaneous Man*. He edited his own Black Ace imprint which published two of Stuart Z. Perkoff's posthumous titles and contributed to that era's irrepressible small press renaissance. Denver's Alan Swallow, New Mexico's Judson Crews, Diane DiPrima and LeRoi Jones (Amiri Baraka) in New York, Lawrence Ferlinghetti, and many others were all extolling the virtues of a new American poetry — anti-institutional, steeped in the vernacular of everyday life, spirited and experimental — that SANG!

Tony believed in community; he believed in a hip, Dionysian, creative-intuitive approach to writing that helped to access his Muse, who was sacred and fundamental to his growth as an artist and writer. His work came up out of the sea, the streets, his friends, he aligned himself with the more rebellious, like-minded, free-

form individuals who relied on each other's counsel and enthusiasm to further their artistic conjurings. After all, he came from Venice, California, a culture of creativity that spawned a beachfront of engaged raconteurs, renegades, writers and artists who found at least a couple of summers worth of magic in the hypnotic give and take of the tides, the climate, which was mostly ideal for living gratuitously just outside of society, and in the spirit of freedom and rebellion from the institutionalized conformist instincts of the desolate 1950's.

Eventually, Tony moved his family to Denver, and lived there off and on, mostly as proprietor of his own bookstores on East Colfax and elsewhere, for 20 years. He was published in many of the classic lit mags and anthologies of the era, *Passion Press, Mile High Underground, The Bowery, Moravagine, Miscellaneous Man, the Croupier, (Sic) Vice & Verse, HARP* and others. He was joined in the late 1960's by poet/publisher James Ryan Morris, editor of *Mile High Underground*, who instituted a series of "total theatre" events that began to shape Denver's nascent literary character. Readings, gallery openings, and theatres were springing up all over town. At one point, he had invited his friends Perkoff and Rios to come to Denver and join him in his bookstore operation, which Perkoff did, with family in tow, upon his release from prison.

As John Arthur Maynard put it in his 1991 book, *Venice West: The Beat Generation in Southern California*: "In the mid-sixties, Scibella had moved to Denver and opened a bookstore; Frankie Rios eventually joined him. According to Scibella, the two of them were making nothing but money. With the hippie thing at its high-water mark, they were even minor celebrities —present at the creation, so to speak. Tony was offering Perkoff a place to live and a one-third interest in the store. The Three Stooges of the Promenade, (Rios, Perkoff and Scibella) would now become the new-and-used-book tycoons of Colfax Avenue."

In 1991, Tony published the first of his eight volume art and poetry anthology Black Ace that ended with a 2007 tribute issue, following his death in Los Angeles in 2003. He published as fertile a roster of literary luminaries as you could find in the firmament of American letters at the end of the century: Jack Kerouac, Neal Cassady, George Herms, Jack Micheline, Charles Bukowski, Diane Di Prima, David Meltzer, Jack Hirschman, Janine Pommy Vega, Michael McClure, Stuart Z. Perkoff, Saul White, John Thomas and many others. Many were friends of his.

On a personal note, I first met Tony when I lived in Denver in the early 1980's when he returned from the coast to open Black Ace Books on Colfax Avenue's "book row." He lived in the back of the store with his second wife, Gayle Davis. As was the tradition, he began to host poetry readings and publication parties. He helped me publish my first book which was a Black Ace/Long Road/Bowery collaboration. I loved and respected Tony because of his passion for the Word, his grace, his loyalties. The pursuit of literary fame and native prizes didn't smolder within him, after experiencing some attention early on. (Although once it was discovered he was back in Denver, he was invited to read in Boulder with Reed Bye, hosted by Andy Clausen, with Anselm Hollo, among others, in attendance.) As he said, reassuringly, in a magazine interview I did with him in Denver in 1986: " . . its that everybody who's tried to do this, everybody that you've never even heard of, that make the whole chain of doing & that fame or something is fate, chance, luck, it doesn't matter, you know, if it wasn't Ginsberg, it'd be somebody else, or what's the difference. So that kinda passes you by . . you have to have that kind of personality to mail stuff out . . after a while you just kinda turn in; it's just you do your work & the rest will take care of itself. Just do your work, She'll take care of you somehow."

Tony had five beautiful children. He was a gambler, loved games of chance and the track. He wrote like people talked. His last two titles, *The Kid in America* and *I'm Afraid There Will be No Parade for Us* were published by Passion Press in Denver in the early 2000's. A small posthumous volume, Retirement Poems was published in New Mexico by Desert Shovel Press in 2005. He had an affinity for working Americans, the laborer, the "oaf" and professed his allegiance often. He devoured pulp westerns, the Sacketts, Dashiell Hammett. He had a great collection of vintage Ace paperbacks. One year, Tony and the artist Steve Wilson had a push-pin, "don't tell know one" art exhibit and reading at a small gallery on South Broadway in Denver. The show featured mostly collage by both artists. He and Wilson served a red, white and blue themed snack array with crackers, assorted processed lunch meats, Velveeta cheese and Cokes. The spread was not without its conscious humor and patriotic irony. The art on the walls was, for the most part, sans frames: bold, brilliant and without borders. I once asked him what the meaning was behind his seemingly defeatist and slightly nihilist-nik mantra "don't tell no one" and he replied: "Because you never know who might show up."

A BRIEF SCIBELLA BIBLIOGRAPHY

Big Trees - *Denver, 1972*

Ace Is Black Of Course - *Denver, 1976*

Turning for Home . . . - *Los Angeles, 1982*

Bowery/West (editor) - *Denver, 1983*

Two For Her (w/Frank Rios) - *Venice, 1989*

Later Poems - *Los Angeles, 1990*

The Kid in America - *Denver, 2000*

I'm Afraid There Will Be No Parade For Us - *Denver, 2002*

A FEW POEMS BY TONY SCIBELLA

Monday here

this is Monday
  lines before me
the first
     poem
is there no excuse
for blunder
   stabbed by the hand
      with pen
so easy

of men
     jungle green
  in rows
of tabulation –
so many for us
too many of them

the sporting news
how unique
  the abstract notion
     today in moderate
     action
        the guerillas
      beat the baboons

theres a tendency to sit
  loaf w/life
see agony every day
   pay no mind
as the news cast flash
the worlds on fire
that's
    endeavors lost

in winds
  nobly considered
    & cast in regrets
then: how is there
   hope in my pocket
are we lonely animals?

never answers:
     only when the worlds
      in flames
    only as the every day
   beats us to dust
    building boxes
     w/no bottoms
      for our possessions.

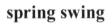

*

spring swing

rain wet
fresh born
the crop seeded
& brite green things shoot for
the sun
lite winks on us

i am weak too
new
colt-like skinny legs
wobble bones in the air
tremble to support my own
weight

chesty
heart-beat
new word world
springtime sattidy nite
fiddle-stringed knife notes
the wired fingers
box blowin

we seek to speak
to all green thumbs
who look to the sun
& feel the rain in the face
moon juice
partial to poets

the ladys tears.

*

in my life, my love

I'm clutching
in my life
my love
as it is the last
to last
not putting silk
on every one
I meet
nor edit
in my mind
whats left
to give
not given

Homage to Pierre Seghers,
French Publisher and Songwriter-Poet (1906-1987)

By Basia Miller

If poetry doesn't help you live, do something else. I consider it to be an essential for man, like the beating of the heart. Pierre Seghers (1)

I OFFER this essay in homage to Pierre Seghers (1906 – 1987), French poet, man of letters and the most important editor and publisher of poetry in France from 1939 to 1969, for his deep commitment, remarkable vision and constant innovation. As I sketch out his life and work, I'll follow the pattern used in Seghers' series on individual poets and comment on his life first, then share two poems that I've translated--a set of song lyrics and a philosophical poem.

It has been eighty years since Seghers first gathered some of his poetry and that of other members of the Resistance such as Paul Eluard and Louis Aragon in an Army-approved collection called *Poètes casqués 39 (Soldier poets 39)*. This was during the drôle de guerre," (2) prior to the June 1940 division into Free France and the Occupation, that is, when the political situation in France was completely uncertain. The magazine later became *Poésie 40 (41, 42, etc.)* but remained identified with the French armies. In an article in *Poésie 40*, the Belgian literary critic André Fontainas stressed its contribution: "The revue is unprecedented in the history of French poetry, because poets, who are often indifferent to each other or compete with each other, have, for the first time, the historic chance to come together and look in the same direction." *https://fr.wikipedia.org/wiki/Pierre_Seghers)*

Though born in Paris of Flemish parents, Seghers had deep roots in the south of France where his family moved when he was young. From 1938 to 1944, his publishing house was in Villeneuve-les-Avignon, in Provence. The poets of the École française" (3) of Avignon approached the challenge of censorship differently than in Paris, where, under the Occupation, poets published their work clandestinely and used pseudonyms. In Free France, they instead adopted a method of indirection borrowed from the medieval troubadors, hiding political allusions under an innocent surface. Their message was always in defense of liberty and against hypocri-

*Pierre Seghers
- Photographer unknown*

Notes:

1. "Si la poésie ne vous aide pas à vivre, faites autre chose. Je la tiens pour essentielle à l'homme autant que les battements de son c?ur." Pierre Seghers

2. The Phoney War, as it is called in English, lasted from September 1939 to May 1940. See https://en.wikipedia.org/wiki/Phoney_War

3. According to Carmody, p. 233, Seghers intended the Poètes casqués to represent the "École Française" (the French School) as "a collective voice, a collective wound, that makes all of us cry out" ("une voix collective, une blessure collective, qui fait crier chacun de nous").

sy. (Carmody, Francis J. "Pierre Seghers, Poet and Editor" (1960)) It's notable that Seghers' initial publications were not inspired by post-war economic expansion or the joy of victory but occured during the war itself. Literature, particularly poetry, joined the battle, before the winner was known. Something for us to think about. Seghers' publishing house represented a kind of literary Resistance, a passionate militancy, that shaped its identity.

In 1944 Seghers moved to Paris, where he founded the series, *Poètes d'aujourd'hui (Contemporary Poets)*, whose initial volume featured Paul Éluard. Seghers chose his poets carefully but inclusively—they varied from well-known to unknown, leading lights to anonymous writers. Some of the American poets that appeared were Tennessee Williams, ee cummings and Langston Hughes. The series eventually included 268 volumes, with print runs in the range of 100,000 to 200,000 copies each.

In his own poetry Pierre Seghers employed an accessible vocabulary and simple forms rather than the learned allusions and stilted syntax that sounded elitist. (Carmody, Francis J. "Pierre Seghers, Poet and Editor" (1960)) Beginning in the 60's he also wrote songs, many of which show the influence of the troubadors. In a rare case where Pierre Seghers' editorial work overlapped with his poetry, he authored his own volume in the *Poètes d'aujourd'hui* series, No. #164 in 1967.

Another step toward inclusivity was taken when in 1952 Seghers began to publish anthologies of literature from other countries, in the series *Autour du monde (Around the World)*. Seghers had traveled widely after the war under the auspices of the French government, as it sought to repair the isolation in which France had been living. The anthologies featured Chinese, African, Hungarian, Swedish, and Spanish poetry, among many others.

When I visited Paris as a student in 1956, books with the Seghers imprint (and its little mermaid emblem), filled the shelves and tables of bookstores along the Boul' Mich. And, fascinating to me, from my rural Kansas background, there were books on tables in the open air ! It's likely they stood out too because Seghers, wanting to appeal to a larger public, published volumes in a paper-back format before the official Livres de poche" were marketed. Soft-covered, almost square and relatively inexpensive, they seemed to invite us to spend our francs in the discovery of French poetry. Looking back at that time, I have to wonder if my experience planted a seed that would lead me, fifty years later, to write poetry.

Seghers had a constant interest in popularizing poetry. He expanded the idea of poetry as an art form to include song lyrics, which he published alongside more traditional poetry as early as 1962. In a 1967 interview, asked whether he preferred to read poetry silently, he said, "No, because [in silence] the word loses its musical quality. The voice gives the work its true dimension, its breath, it brings out resonances and ruptures, the whole palette of language… Poetry sometimes prefers to travel from mouth to ear." (Interview with Pierre Seghers by Gabrielle Rolin for *Le Monde*)

Seghers' innovations, some minor, like dedicating a volume to a poet whose name is unknown, and others that horrified traditionalists, like including song lyrics in books of poetry, seem somehow to reflect his family's artisanal origins. His grandfather was a cabinet-maker and his father as well, before the latter created photographic papers for the new field of photography. Seghers says, in a 1972 interview, "the atmosphere of the printing house, the pleasure of correcting proofs on marble, even the manufacture of a collection, the joy of the worker, of the artisan, you never forget these. You either have it in your heart or not. One is never cured of poetry." (Interview with Pierre Seghers by Jean-Luc Maxence) His family's craft tradition seems to underlie Pierre

Seghers' pleasures in publishing poetry.

Seghers sold his publishing house in 1969, leaving him "completely on the other side." (Personal letter to Francine Caron) During the mid-seventies, he translated Hafiz (14th century) and Omar Khayyam (11-12th century), knowing that the method of allusion used by the Persian poets to protect themselves from political attacks resembled the stylistic techniques of the 1939 "École française."

At the age of 68, Seghers wrote a dissertation, "Poetry in France and popular culture," at the Université de Paris-X, near Versailles. He meant it to reflect his belief that poetry changes people's lives, but, characteristically, he considered the doctorate a simple passport that would allow him to open more doors. (Interview with Pierre Seghers by Jacques Chancel)

In 1983, at the request of Jacques Chirac, mayor of Paris at the time, Seghers established La Maison de la Poésie de la Ville de Paris (the House of Poetry of the City of Paris), which offers a full program of readings, lectures and festivals.

Throughout his life, though he worked in Paris, Pierre Seghers would return to Provence four months a year, loving the silence and the respect for handcrafts. (Interview with Pierre Seghers by Jacques Chancel)

Now I'd like to share some of Pierre Seghers' own writing. He was a prolific writer, producing plays, song lyrics and poems throughout his life, but, as noted on one of the YouTube albums, "it is rare to find people who know that this honorable man also wrote." (Kilian Rochat, actor and director of the video.) The first is a set of song lyrics from a volume published posthumously, *Derniers écrits (Last Writings)*. The philosophical poem, from a 1981 collection, *Fortune, Infortune Fort Une*, is interesting because the double 8-syllable lines, retained in the English translation, are reminiscent of song lyrics, though the subject-matter is profoundly serious.

Fireflies

He who doesn't know fireflies
does not know his own life. The immensity of the
    nights falls
on the tall grasses and flowers, the high sheaves of
    shadow, where,
muted by day, countless clusters now sparkle, a dance
    of moments

Seeds of suns scattered haphazardly at the festival
On the slopes of the hills, spangles from a masked ball.

Tell me, my life, who are we? O Ephemeral ones,
    where are we?
Extinguished flecks of gold, life and its scenes in
    movement

    «Les Lucioles» by Pierre Seghers
    Translation by Basia Miller

Les Lucioles

Qui ne connaît pas les lucioles
ne connaît pas sa propre vie. L'immensité des nuits
    descend
dans les hautes herbes et les fleurs, hautes grappes
    d'ombre où scintillent
les innombrables girandoles que le jour tue, un bal
    d'instants

Grains de soleils éparpillés jetés aux hasards de la fête
Sur les cambrures des collines, les paillettes d'un bal
    masqué

Dis-moi – ma vie, qui sommes-nous? Où en sommes-
    nous Ephémères?
Points d'or éteints, regards et vie en movement.

    Pierre Seghers

I Live Like a Hidden Treasure

I live like a hidden treasure ever burning to know itself
I am a light on the inside carried uselessly, which
    dazzles
I am transparent and muddled ; and who spoke of
    an amalgam,
Of a desperate alchemy, those ruts in a trail of folly?

I am a fragile bag of skin, an ordering of miracles--
The timers and regulators that will unexpectedly stop
The mechanism of fluids and deep springs that will
    always run
toward other unquenchable thirsts. And now I ask,
    where, O where, shall

one live life and its meanders like a pilgrim on his
    journey
blinded now and then by lanterns ? To each his
    own. They will move past
As their fiery eyes pierce the gloom, perhaps they
    will discover me
To touch me and, indifferent, see me delivered from
    this hole.

What if the Cosmos were a man and man only a
    tiny speck
that ricochets from dune to wave, dying and again
    surviving
for eons, cast there by mercy or by chance, just an
    irony
a wretched whisper of matter, ephemeral, corroding all ?

Mirrors are enemies of mine. Life is an inverted
    image
at the border of the Nothing, which is the All. I ebb
    and flow
I'm the ash of an energy, a bubble of foam still
    bursting
age after age. I'm just trying to report what we are.
    That's all.

    «Je vis comme…» by Pierre Seghers
    Translation by Basia Miller

Je vis comme un trésor caché

Je vis comme un trésor caché qui brûle en lui de se
    connaître
Je suis lueur à l'intérieur en vain portée, qui éblouit
Je suis distinct et confondu ; et qui parlait d'un
    amalgame,
D'une alchimie désespérée, les ornières d'un chemin fou ?

Je suis un sac de peau fragile, un agencement de miracles
Des chronomètres, des compteurs qui vont s'arrêter
    tout à coup
Une mécanique de fluides et des sources intarissables
qui s'en iront vers d'autres soifs jamais étanchées.
    Où, mais où

vivre la vie dans ses détours comme un pèlerin sur
    sa piste
aveuglé parfois par des phares ? Chacun les siens.
    Ils passeront
Leurs yeux de feu perçant l'obscur, ils me
    découvriront peut-être
pour m'extraire et pour m'emporter, sans l'avoir
    voulu, hors du trou.

Si l'Univers n'était qu'un homme et l'homme une
    parcelle infime
qui ricoche de dunes en vagues, meurt et survit,
    siècles d'instants
jeté là par miséricorde ou par hasard, une ironie
un frôlement de la matière, éphémère et corrodant tout ?

Les miroirs me sont ennemis. La vie est une image
    inverse
au seuil du Rien qui est le Tout. Je suis un flux qui
    vient et va
L'escarbille d'une énergie, un grain d'écume qui déferle
de millénaire en millénaire. Je cherche à nous dire.
    C'est tout.

    Pierre Seghers

Pierre Seghers, no. 17 in Fortune, Infortune,
Fort Une *Reprinted with permission.*

Sources

These are the full citations for references in the article, along with a few other useful sources. If no source is specifically cited in the article, the information is from the detailed French Wikipedia entry for Pierre Seghers. Except for the Carmody reference, all are in French. All translations are mine.

Burin, André. Interview with Pierre Seghers, "La poésie pour qui?" 1969. https://www.ina.fr/video/CPF10005622

Carmody, Francis J. "Pierre Seghers, Poet and Editor." *Books Abroad* 34, no. 3 (1960): 233-35. *https://www.jstor.org/stable/40114774?seq=1#page_scan_tab_contents*

Chancel, Jacques. Interview with Pierre Seghers, "Radioscopies," France Inter, 1977. *https://www.youtube.com/watch?v=IhlvwznDWPQ.*

Letter from Pierre Seghers to Francine Caron June 14, 1978 (private collection)

Maxence, Jean-Luc. Interview with Pierre Seghers, 1972 for Rebelle(s) Mag. *https://rebelles-lemag.com/2016/12/16/1972-interview-de-pierre-seghers/*

"Poètes en résistance," Ministère de l'éducation nationale, Paris. *https://www.reseau-canope.fr/poetes-en-resistance/accueil/*

Rochat, Kilian, actor and director of video in which he reads selected lyrics from *Pierre Seghers, Derniers écrits*, 2002. *https://www.youtube.com/watch?v=gmbh5-O16h0.*

Rolin, Gabrielle in Le Monde. Interview with Pierre Seghers, 1967. *https://www.lemonde.fr/archives/article/1967/08/23/entretien-avec-pierre-seghers-poete-et-editeur-de-poetes_2606314_1819218.html?xtmc=entretien_editeur&xtcr=2*

Wikipedia entry: Pierre Seghers. *https://fr.wikipedia.org/wiki/Pierre_Seghers*

EATING AND DRINKING WITH THE BEATS (PART ONE)
by Charles Plymell

AFTER THE famous Gough St. bash where the Beats met the Hippies, Allen invited me over for a light dinner. He was just back from India trying to get Neal settled in, and Peter, and Anne. They later shared the Gough St. flat with me. Allen was staying with his old friend from the beat days, "Dr. Radar", who lived just down the hill from Ferlinghetti. A few days earlier we had visited Larry at his house, ate some salad Larry made, and some cheese and wine. Larry liked good French wine. Radar had a monkey in his yard. Allen said I had to go through the "Monkey Test," whatever that was. He told me it would bite if it sensed the wrong aura. I passed the test. Allen had gone shopping in North Beach with

Larry and had bought some caviar, wine, fruit and cheese. He asked me if I liked caviar. I didn't. He had some dark bread to put it on. We pieced around and drank some wine and rolled a joint. He told me about his Indian travels and asked me about McClure and some other poets from Kansas. Peter came to the door and walked right past the monkey. Allen said he would come over to the Gough St. flat and bring some poems for a little mag I was doing, called "Now." Both Mike and Allen had written a poem to each other, a kind of apology to each other to set the tone for the new "love" generation. Bruce Conners, an artist from Wichita, would soon paint LOVE in street lettering in the lane where Oak St. turned onto the freeway. I formed my lasting impression of Allen Ginsberg: He came to make history.

It was Thanksgiving dinner at 1403 Gough St.,1963 just after the Kennedy assassination when Robert LaVigne dropped by, talked to Ginsberg, who was tidying up the kitchen. Robert spotted dirt on the floor and wiped it clean, making a point to Allen, who had lived in the flat in the 50's and had taken Robert's love, Peter. Later that day was the big dinner in the dining room. Neal Cassady was rolling a joint from his shoe box lid, telling stories, while Anne and others were planning the traditional Thanksgiving meal. As the day grew late, several others confounded the cooking. Old Frank, my sister Betty's husband, who got me a job on the docks, was telling his stories of the wild early west about his being the offspring of the Sheriff of Deadwood, South Dakota and a Black madam. The scene was somewhat gloomy, as it had been overcast for several days, but still pleasant and traditionally reverent. Someone off the street had happened by and was included in the meal. There were lots of drinks and Peter Orlovsky insisted on doing the dishes; he obsessively washed everything.

It was at "Foster Fudds" (Foster's cafeteria) just below the Hotel Wentley the same year when I grabbed a naked lunch with Ginsberg and Leary before going to a party. The talk was serious, concerning contraband and the law. Leary had just come from Big Sur where he visited Bob Branaman, who had cooked him a Kansas stew.

At Mike's Pool Hall in North Beach Pam and I ate fantastic minestrone and Salami sandwiches on sourdough bread. The salami factory was next door. Pam was 17 years old, so it helped when Larry was with us. In those days, the old Italian men sat at the checkered table cloths and played Caruso on the juke box as they studied the pool players. Pam and I then went over to City Light's basement to look over a manuscript Ferlinghetti was going to publish. Later I joined Whalen and Ginsberg for a photo in what was to become Kerouac Alley.

Allen, Neal, Anne and I had planned a trip to Bolinas to see another friend of mine from Lawrence, Karen Wright, who had visited Gough St. to play Dylan's "Blowing in the Wind" for us for the first time. Neal had been fighting with Anne and jumped in his '39 Pontiac ready to drive. As we rounded the coastal hills and curves, Neal began gearing down the car with the stick shift hitting second gear to slow down while pulling the emergency brake (as it was called in those days) with one hand and slapping Anne with the other. He informed us that the brakes on the car were out. Allen prudently advised him to slow down, but this made him drive faster. Allen and I were being tossed around in the back seat like two Marx Brothers extras. Allen managed to get out his camera and took the famous photo of Neal, eyes off the road, head turned to Anne, cursing: the shot with the torn headliner of the Pontiac above Neal. We stopped at a snack shop where I snapped a photo. Neal liked junk food because he usually wasn't "meal hungry" on speed. When we arrived, Neal spotted a copy of *On The Road* and a comfortable chair and began reading dramatically. Karen fixed a Guacamole dip and Mexican dinner using just ripe black Avocados from the lower San Joaquin.

In 1966, Allen Ginsberg came to Wichita in his VW camper, Peter driving and taking care of brother Julius. I told them to meet me downtown at the crossroad of America, at Main and Douglas where 50's hoodlum hipsters used to score criscross Benzedrine and lounge-lizards bopped the night train in. By the time I arrived, Allen and Peter had found metropolitanism at the Chinese restaurant where petty gangsters hung out. Allen was delighted to walk down old cowtown streets past the pawnshops, barbecue joints R&B race music dives and cowboy honky-tonks. We spent hours drinking at Okie's bar, swilling up the 3.2 beer and blues. Orlovsky sang and drank and yodeled. He was very much into real tearjerker hillbilly pathos. We went to Chances R where Glenn Todd recorded a scene from a visit in '63 in a story he wrote at the time and later found. I've included a section from it in his postscript.

Robert Frank and his film assistant landed at the Wichita airport. Next to Okie's bar was the seedy old Hotel Eaton with a stained decor of decadent elegance, which remains to this day as it turned into a elegant flophouse for the poor. Robert took photos of the large oil painting of Carry Nation above a bar she had axed. Past the marbled registry was an attended elevator and a sleepy elevator operator. The elevator has old folding-caged doors. Beyond it were the urinals and marbled sinks. Next to that was the "all night long" café where dejected hillbillies and old blues sax players ate. It is written about in Pat O'Connor's, "*Moody's Skidrow Beanery.*" Here you could get chops and even chicken-fried steak, an awful Kansas favorite of the old timers. To us, the greatest thing on the menu was a real Kansas breakfast, from biscuits to steaks and pancakes with eggs on top of them, bacon, home fries peppered and catsupped. It was a good "wee hours" breakfast place after one had been drunk and back again halfway sober and tingly but tired from hangin' an' bangin' one's chops and thighs all night long.

Summer 1967, Pam and I, Janine Pommy Vega and Herbert Huncke stopped in a diner on the way to the clinic in Northern California where Gerry Garcia later died; we were to take Huncke there to clean up. At the diner Huncke ordered pancakes and poured a lot of junk-sick syrup on them. He then looked blank, went on the nod as his face fell into the plate of pancakes. He recovered, looked at the waitress and the customers and said. "I bet you all think I'm crazy. Well I am!"

It was a year later when Robert Crumb moved to San Francisco and Don Donahue came over to our flat on Post St. where Pam and I had an antique Multilith. I showed Don how Robert would have to draw color overlays for us to print the color cover of the original ZAP. The pages were designed to do the maximum size for the old Multi [Multilith printer] and were printed on newsprint.

There were many copies destroyed in the printing, adding perhaps to its thousand dollars value at Sotheby's decades later. That night we went to Crumb's apartment to collate the comix, where his wife, Dana, later the cookbook author, made us a Crumb cake with a cartoon icing.

By 1968, Pam and I were in London and visited Burroughs at his 8 Duke Street flat. He had written me a cut up of some poems of mine and others in the second issue of *Now*, titled *Now Now* with lettering by Branaman of bodies in sex. I wrote the following poem:

8 DUKE ST., LONDON, 1968

In London in a very neat
and sensible flat,
lives the genius
of contemporary American prose.
More like a poet
he veers and speaks both
naturally and subliminally.
More like a medium
he chats pleasantly
from a space apart
or from a chamber
of spirits disguised
in an everyday world.
A tall man, slightly stooped
from the weight of all
combinations and formulas
of all possible plots,
Mr. Burroughs rises
and leans against the window ledge
. . . could have been a St. Louis
merchant or farmer
about to speculate on the weather.
"Those birds," he says, gesturing out
the window to a flock that caught his fancy:
"in the mornings they fly one way
and in the evenings they
fly back the other way."
And with that he reached for his hat
and we went to the local pub for brandy.

End of the summer of '68, Pam and I met Allen in NYC and went with him to the William F. Buckley show, "Firing Line." Ed Sanders and Jack Kerouac met us there. Kerouac was doing a show with him as two Republicans discussing the Viet Nam War. Kerouac said it was a conspiracy between the North and South Vietnamese to get more American Jeeps over there. He then made some remarks about Jews referring to Ginsberg in the audience. As we left, I was behind Kerouac walking past Truman Capote's dressing room door, opened for trolling. Someone said there's Truman Capote. Kerouac turned around saying "Where is that little queer, I've been wanting to......." At that point a crowd gathered in his dressing room and the encounter ended amicably, if not humorously. As we went down the stairs, Kerouac grabbed me by the collar and said something like "who do you think you are...?" I shoved him against the wall and said something about the same. Allen acted typically, both woeful and excited by the action. We then went to a nearby bar and sat for a long while, Jack drinking hard liquor, sitting next to Allen and Pam, animated, talking seriously about things I don't recall. I sat in the booth on the other side of the table with two men who were with Kerouac, not saying much, eating fries and drinking beer. Later I learned that this was the last time Allen and Jack saw each other.

We were on our way to Cherry Valley with Allen and stopped at the Big Pink's House where they were assembling for a Jam. It was a big pink suburban-type ranch house. I wrote the following poem:

AT THE BIG PINK'S HOUSE

They came from the city,
from the hills around
Pittsburgh... Amarillo.
One packed a lunch
drove a Hudson Hornet
and the music sure was good.

The house had vinyl pink siding,
big front room for the band.
The women made lunch.
We ate near a large rock,
drinking good scotch,
enjoying mystic truth's smooch

the music sure was good.

A subtle smoke beyond the brain
invoked an Indian ghost over the lake
and floated into the rising full moon.

That night we left with bard and harmonium
drove to Cherry Valley and Kansas across states
that didn't matter anymore on to San Francisco.

We stayed at Allen's farm in Cherry Valley and ate borsch and fresh vegetable dinner made from some of the vegetables Peter had brought in from the garden. To entertain Elizabeth, Allen played some of his Blake songs on the antique organ he had.

In the bucolic hills of Cherry Valley *Reality Sandwiches* and *Kaddish* were being translated into French by Mary Beach and Claude Pélieu. There were many transients staying at the poor little isolated farmhouse, so cooking outside was helpful. Usually the fare was whatever anyone thoughtful happened to bring from town. The cooking was primitive and sanitary conditions didn't prevail. The water source was below the cabin and an outhouse was uphill. Expensive cooking ware was abundant, however, as were many anachronisms at the farm. Most were alleged vegetarians or had haphazard new-aged diets; although, it was rumored that Peter ate steak on the sly when he made trips to town. He had a pet pig, which grew to 600 lbs. and shared Peter's bed when the weather was cold. When Peter left the farm, he gave the pig to someone on condition that it wouldn't be eaten. It wasn't long before someone said it had been hit by a car. Things weren't always as reverent as the setting. Corso and Orlovsky were always fighting, mainly because Corso wanted to roast the pig, and Pélieu was talking about everyone in disdain and disgust, especially when they were naked in the pond, calling Corso "Zucchini Face" and the like. Claude and Mary did "miraculously" transform some garden vegetables into a great French vinaigrette salad that Allen exclaimed as the best he had eaten and why couldn't Peter do that, etc.

In 1975, James Grauerholtz, John Giorno, and William Burroughs came to dinner at our house in Cherry Valley, which is now the "Rose and Kettle Restaurant." Pam had gone out of her way to fix Texas Barbeque Ribs, for Bill's recollections of his Texas "farming days." She had to special order the long ribs because we couldn't buy them in Yankee country. I hand made potato chips, slicing each one keenly with a butcher knife at Bill's interest. We had Vodka for him, of course and the rest of us drank Carlsberg's Elephant Ale, a favorite of mine. Orlovsky came down from the East Hill "Committee on Poetry" farm to eat with us. He was lamenting one of his Guru's ill health, and pressed Bill for his feelings. Burroughs snarled, "I don't give a shit if he lives or dies!" Later Burroughs prowled the house selecting a bedroom, checking out my empty Percodan bottle, placing it back on the shelf with a Hmmph! The next day we went up to the farm's pond and Peter stripped and jumped in to exhibit a Tarzan swim.

Sometime later, Janine Pommy Vega and Allen came to dinner at the same place, Allen in his farmer's overalls. We had a big garden and our daughter, Elizabeth helped us gather the vegetables.

Gerard Malanga came to dinner and showed Pam how to make a vinaigrette, which she still makes for salads. Carl Solomon and Ray Bremser used to sit on the porch and watch the action in downtown Cherry Valley and tell fishing stories. Ray and I made our daily trips to the local drugstore and then to Cooperstown to get our daily bottles of Turpin Hydrate and Codeine and a six-pack of cheap beer for Ray.

During that time I went with Anne Waldman, Ginsberg and Burroughs to Montreal for a "counter-culture" reading at the Biblioteque Nationale. Bill started with cocktails, not wanting to eat heavy before going on stage. He ordered a Vodka, and I, never knowing quite what to drink, ordered the same. He quickly changed his order? After dinner was served, Allen ordered a glass of milk. Burroughs angrily reprimanded him for it and said he shouldn't have that; it would fuck up his vocal chords on stage. We met Mary Beach and Claude Pélieu there. Claude immediately made enemies refusing to speak French. The organizers had pegged him as a CIA agent. The whole reading turned into a farce, Allen and Anne putting the best face on it. Allen visited with Emmett Grogan. Claude saw all of the "counter-culture" as bullshit and put down the Quebecquois. I hopped a bus and returned to Cherry Valley writing the following poem:

OH BONY ROBOT DRIVER

Take me to the hard jackpot
to the vacant house, the hill and the riverbank
Then pour some gravity
On the wheels to
Just glide around the corners.

I got way down blue inside
that day,
drove west out of Albany...
Toward a stretch of valleys
and high hills.

Like in the western states
that scarred their sunsets in me
many times before,
bottle at my feet,
red dirt canyon rim.

Back home the cold mountain hangs still.
I slipped into my longjohns,
put on my earphones
lay back in a foam rubber flight.

Put on a record of Hank Williams' blues
Confessed to a tune I didn't want to hear.

And I didn't know
where the magnetized needle

would take the full moon
burning outside my window.
Maybe a slight reading of biorhythms
would produce a flight pattern
into that milkweed sleeve
the crimson sunset lined against the space where I
could not aim my gliding flocks of memory . . . .

To be continued in LUMMOX 9 (2020).

LIVING ON THE EDGE
by Coco Ramirez

I WAS nine years old when I first attempted to end my own life. There was so much abuse and trauma that I had already faced, so by this point I wanted out. If what my life had been thus far is what I could expect of the world, then I didn't want to have a life beyond age nine.

Hospitalized from age two to four for non-cancerous tumors within my throat and left ear. Two years of my developing brain and life spent listening to the sounds of survival monitored recovery. I lived in and out of the hospital for most of my existence. To this day the cold antiseptic and sterile smells of the hospital comfort me like fresh warm linens out of the dryer. As time progressed nothing and no one felt as secure as my hospital room.

Raped and molested by family members. Coerced into sexual acts by older cousins on both side of my family. Uncles would have me sit on their laps while fondling beneath my clothes. Car rides with my Uncles were never without them swallowing my face, tongue in my mouth, taste of cigarettes and beer while grabbing my breast. It was either me or my sister Cassie, so I made certain it was always me.

You don't get over it you know. It haunts you. Torments you. Every minuscule detail of every event. Having to attend family functions and holidays with a straight face left me queasy and frightened. Faces I had come to know and trust circle like harpies. They take their time one by one, feasting on my innocence. Here time slows, it crawls, it stretches like tar. There is no escaping these ravaging beast. The torment of hands exploring the hidden treasures of my humanity. Sequestered on an isle from which joy will never escape.

I broke one of my Grandmother's figurines on a night my parents left me to spend the night there. My cousin of course was there too, a witness to my *crime*. "I won't tell Grandma if you do this favor for me." I can still see the figurine in his hands in two parts with him mimicking putting them back together. Snapped into two pieces that would never be whole again and neither would I.

"You don't want to get in trouble do you?" No kid ever wants to get in trouble. He of course had to add "your parents will be so mad" and with that I found myself laying flat on my back, legs spread as he forced himself inside me. "Ssshhh, don't make any noise" as he placed his hand over my mouth to quite my whimpering cries.

There was no escape. Trips to grandmas or trips to my aunts' houses, my aggressors were everywhere. My other cousin would hide me in his closet and fondle my barely pubescent body. Why does this keep happening to me? What am I doing wrong I would think to myself. Cassie of course was always spared since I made sure no one ever came near her.

It just got to be too much for my developing brain to handle and process. All I could think of was how I felt inside. Microscopic and invisible parasites squirming and worming around underneath my flesh. Flashbacks, foresight, nothing, everything, everywhere there was no escape. I wanted no part of me to be left.

It was spring and we were getting ready for Easter. As Mom, Dad, and Cass got ready inside the house I escaped out the side kitchen door. There in the driveway I snuck quietly into Dad's 1968 Chrysler Station Wagon. Took the red lighter he had stashed in the front console and readied to light myself on fire.

A small bottle of lighter fluid sat conveniently next to the red lighter. Although it was springtime and everyone else was in bright festive colors, I insisted on wearing my black velvet dress with a white lace trim on the bottom part of the skirt. Dousing myself in fluid preparing to meet my end my little sister Cassie peered from the front lawn. I was just about to click the silver spindle of fate when her voice startled me.

Inquisitively in her white sun hat and colorful flower-patterned dress she approached me. "What are you doing?" I could tell she was scared, nervously awaiting an answer. As I spun around surprised at her catching me in the act mere seconds before I could light the lighter, I pause. *I'm going to light myself on fire.* There was no sorrow in my words. No fear held me back, the sheer determination left my reply like a 120-pound dead weight dropped in front of her.

Powerless tears streamed down her soft brown cheeks. "I'm going to tell" was all she could muster up to try and stop me from fulfilling my plan. Cass begged me not to leave her alone. Sobbing in my arms the smell of kerosene made no difference in how tight she held onto me. How could I now go through with this? My then five-year-old sister needed me.

Who would protect her innocence from the demons and dark cold places of this world? Although it was torturous to abandon my only salvation the pain in her eyes burned so much hotter than the flames, I hoped would consume me. Thinking that her pleas of distress in being alone were not enough she just kept repeating that she would tell our parents and demanded I promise I would never leave her.

In my mind I knew that by the time she went in and came back out with them was more than enough time to end my own life. Still her words pierced straight through the pain like a bolt of lightning. Her love for me jolted me back to this plane of existence where she "needed" me. I promised her that I would never leave her side.

I apologized for being selfish and not thinking how my actions would affect her. Kids! We were merely kids! With nothing but the love we had for each other to hold us together.

Times were much more different back then.

Child services was not what it is today. My parents after that event decided to take me to my first of many therapists.

My Mom to her dying day never believed me when I told her and the therapist what happened. Mom was convinced it was my Father's doing and that he somehow tricked my brain into it being someone else. Dad was no better in stating that "you must have asked for it". When Dad had one to many, he would call me a whore. These are just small remembrances of my childhood into adolescence's.

I secluded myself from anyone who was not my sister through school, but that didn't really keep the trauma at bay. Date raped at sixteen. Sexually harassed at my first job by the age of seventeen. No matter how baggy I wore my clothes or how many sweaters I put on it made zero difference.

After high school the abuse would continue to stack itself taller than the leaning tower of Pisa. My foundation of self just as unstable and marsh like inside. Indeed, I too would live in "*The Field of Miracles*" as doctors, psychologist and psychiatrist would marvel at how I was still alive after all the abuse and trauma. Verbal abuse, domestic abuse, with my parents still siding with I must be doing something wrong. "Just do what you're told and don't talk back" mom would say.

My first husband beat me frequently, leaving six stitches in my head by hitting me with a cordless phone. Later after I made the bold decision to leave, he would intentionally hit me with our car, two-year-old at the time in the back seat. Sandwiched between his car and mine fracturing my pelvic bone behind the elementary school where I was dropping off lunch to our five-year-old.

It has never ended for me. Trauma after trauma. Blow after blow of mental anguish. My most recent employer sending me overboard with his intentional inflection of emotional distress. Up the elevator to the second floor Psychologist office. Through the double doors that section off the "mental wellness" branch of the hospital I check in at the desk. I am handed a tablet with questions highlighting how I am feeling currently. Questions of day to day activities and the ever so famous…" *Are you suicidal today?"*

When I enter the office, I take a seat brooding and desperately trying to keep myself together. I can feel the rage behind my eyes. I can taste the sour desperation in my mouth. Then it comes…" Is there a plan to end your life?" Are you kidding me?!?! Of course there is a plan! There is always a plan! I answer as if I was being asked what color the sky was. "Well can you share with me how you have considered ending your life?" I scoff at the lunacy of the question.

Hand on my forehead with my other arm crossed over my breast I answer slowly. Stifled breath, hand extended I motion to everything in the room and say anything and everything is a means to end your life. "Yes, but have you planned anything more specific?" Good God are these people that slow? How are these trained professionals supposed to help me if they can't tell just how close to the edge I am standing!

Okay, breathe in, breath out, you want all the gory details, do you? I begin to list the various plans I have thought out and planned over the years:

• Jump off the Lake bridge in front of the Gold line and ensure the doctor knows yes, I have sat and timed how long it would take to fall just right before it hits
• Step in front of a moving vehicle
• Place rocks in my pockets and jump off the pier into the ocean
• Overdose on my medication
• Slit my writs
• A plastic bag over my head
• My neck hanging from a tree

I list them all at machine gun speed. Do you get how much I don't want to be here anymore? Do you understand that I can't take anymore trauma in my life? Do you understand I am placing my life in your hands and that's why I brought myself here!

I'm stopped before I can list every way that I've thought of and asked, "is there intent to follow through with it?" Red faced, out of breath, hyperventilating an answer with a river of tears soaking my face and blouse…*no, I reply. I promised my sister.*

Memories of Hubert "Cubby" Selby
by M. G. Stephens

I WAS in a rehab, drying out from drugs and alcohol and I received a call, something we were not supposed to have, and when I answered the telephone in the little booth where we were allowed to speak on the telephone, I heard the familiar laugh of my old friend and mentor Hubert "Cubby" Selby, the author of Last Exit to Brooklyn and many other great American contemporary classics. They were shooting the film of the novel, first in Germany, and later in Brooklyn. Selby was in New York for the film shoot. He had called my apartment on 110th Street and my then wife told him where I was. I have no idea how he was able to penetrate the ironclad rule of no outside calls—we could only call out during certain hours of the day— and get through to me or how they allowed me to take the call during one of therapy sessions upstairs at the old Billy Rose mansion in the East 90s between Park and Lexington avenues. In those days, 1988, the Smithers alcohol treatment center was housed in that gaudy house, but later was sold off and the rehab re-housed at Roosevelt Hospital on the Upper West Side.

Selby had a laugh that was maniacal, diabolical, and plainly insane; it was unmistakable and unique, sui generis, as they say. When he spoke, he would throw back his head and open his mouth and let that laugh fly out. It was both beautiful and scary.

I told Cubby that I had hit bottom.

That's what made him laugh again.

"Mike," he said, "every bottom has a trap-door."

I would never forget that statement.

When I thought I had this disease of alcoholism licked, I would remember Selby's remark: every bottom had a trap door.

Back in the late 1960s, my friend Ross Feld had taken my novel Gulfweed Voices to Grove Press where he worked in the editorial department as the poet and novelist Gilbert Sorrentino's assistant. Gil had liked the novel and even wanted to publish it, but he explained to me how long and arduous the process was at Grove to get a book taken on by the publisher Barney Rossett.

"You may be an old man by the time they publish this book," he said.

But I had always wanted to publish a book with Grove Press because they published some of my favorite writers, including Samuel Beckett, who had changed my life when I first read his novels (Molloy, Malone Dies, and The Unnamable) when I was fifteen years old. They also published Jean Genet and William Burroughs, Jack Kerouac and Irving Rosenthal, not to mention the bible for all young American poets in the 1960s, New American Poetry edited by Donald Allen. But my favorite writer of all was Hubert Selby and his great American novel, Last Exit to Brooklyn, which Grove had published in 1964 when I was an impressionable undergraduate at a state university in upstate New York. It had changed my life even more than reading Beckett had when I was fifteen. I was eighteen years old when I first read Selby.

I would learn from Sorrentino that he and Selby were childhood friends out a Bay Ridge neighborhood in Brooklyn, that Cubby had been a football player and a tough guy, and then had shipped out on a freighter, where he became ill with tuberculosis. He had one of his lungs removed at a hospital in Germany, then became addicted to morphine during his recuperation. According to my friends in the various downtown bars where I hung out, Cubby was a heroin addict and he lived in Los Angeles.

At the time, I was under arrest for being the accessory to a drug crime in New Hampshire. I had been at the MacDowell Colony in Peterborough and volunteered one evening to go to the Keene airport to pick up the novelist Rudy Wurlitzer, who was flying back to the colony from Hollywood. I drove there with a painter named Ken. Unbeknownst to us, a cop followed the car. We had gotten lost and pulled into a gas station for directions to the airport. By our look—long hair, beards, hippie clothing—we were immediately suspicious characters, so when Rudy hopped off the plane, the cop arrested all three of us.

There was no probable cause, only this cop's prejudiced instinct towards people who seemed different than what he knew. At the police station he informed us that the week before he had busted Country Joe and the Fish for drug possession, so he was certain he was going to find something on us. I didn't have anything on me, nor did Ken, but Rudy did, so we all got locked up.

At the time, the Vietnam War was going great guns after the 1968 Tet Offensive, and I was immediately drafted into the military upon arrival back in New York. I was apparently the youngest person ever admitted to the MacDowell Colony (twenty-one at the time), and now was the youngest one ever thrown out of there. After one day in the military I was sent back to New York because I couldn't be drafted while my court case was still active. I was told to return to Fort Dix in New Jersey after the outcome of the trial was resolved.

That autumn my girlfriend and I took a train to San Francisco from New York, and after a few months there, we hitch-hiked south to Los Angeles. We stayed with the sculptor Ardison Phillips in his downtown LA loft. Earlier in 1968, he had stayed in our apartment in New York, well, not really my apartment, but my girlfriend's place. He was a great foodie, even then, making spectacular meals for everyone. Later he would become renowned for his restaurant, the Studio Café, one of the hot spots in Los Angeles.

My girlfriend borrowed her brother's car and we drove to West Hollywood to meet Hubert Selby, the visit set up by Gil Sorrentino. Selby told me to meet him at Barney's Beanery on Holloway near Santa Monica

"Cubby" Selby - Photographer unknown

Boulevard. We spent the evening drinking and talking and then wound up at his kitchen table nearby. Eventually his wife told him that he needed to sleep. She told me: "What he won't tell you is that he's a diabetic, he shouldn't be drinking, he needs his sleep, and he only has one lung." She paused. "Plus he just getting off of heroin, and he shouldn't be drinking so goddamn much, it's bad for his liver." Suzanne, his wife, instructed me and my friend to go home.

"Come back this evening," Selby said, and we did.

We met a few more times that trip, and then my girlfriend and I went back to San Francisco.

I began corresponding with Cubby from that point onwards until his death forty years later.

A few months after we had that couple of days binge drinking, Selby got sober; I think it was in April 1969. I didn't get sober until 1988.

Selby's second novel The Room was written as a direct result of how the LA police had treated him when he was a drug addict. At the time in Los Angeles, it was a felony to be high on heroin, and that's what had happened to Selby. He had gone into a diabetic coma while incarcerated and nearly died. At his court hearing, the judge would ask him a question and Selby, deeply under the influence of Herman Melville's Bartleby the Scrivener would answer, "I would prefer not to." At least that is how he told the story to me. Eventually he would get clear of the various charges, get clean of heroin and then alcohol, and live clean and sober for the rest of his life. Of course, it was not a happily ever after story. He struggled financially most of his life, working odd jobs in West Hollywood where he lived. He had been a gas station pump jockey and a script reader, among other things, barely making ends meet. Once upon a time he had earned a lot of money from Last Exit to Brooklyn, but during his drug years, all that money disappeared into his veins. It was not until the

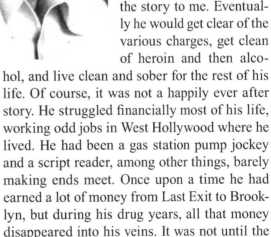

very end of his life that he began to earn a living from his writing, and that was mainly from the movies that were made of Last Exit and Requiem for a Dream. In Germany, his novel The Willow Tree was a best seller, and that helped ease his burden too in the early Noughties.

At some point in the late 70s Selby moved back to New York and lived briefly and improbably in Greenwich, Connecticut. But that did not work out for him. I remember his giving a reading at the Tin Palace bar on the Bowery, and how exciting it was to see him in New York again, and later, I was in graduate school at Yale, and he drove over to see a performance of my play Cloud Dream. Earlier in the 70s I had been friends with the novelist Richard Price, who was also a Selby protégé, and Selby would speak about Richie. I think he was hoping to have a success similar to Price's, but other than his first novel, the other books never sold in quite that way. Eventually Selby returned to LA and would live there, now single, for the rest of his life.

In the late 1980s, I was teaching for about five years at Princeton University in their creative writing program. At one point I was on a panel with Joyce Carol Oates, Russell Banks, Toni Morrison, and Paul Auster to discuss the American novel or some such topic. I remember being asked who had written, in my estimate, the great American novel of our time. I can't remember most of the answers now, but I do recall that I said that Hubert Selby's Last Exit to Brooklyn was the great novel for me of the 20th century. I am not going to suggest that my job at Princeton was shortened by that remark, but it was obvious that these literary titans did not agree with what I said.

Yet Selby was unique among American writers. His influences were writers such as Herman Melville and Isaac Babel. His own mentor had been his childhood friend Gilbert Sorrentino, a key figure in the downtown alternative poetry scene in the late 1950s and early 1960s. Sorrentino then had gone on to create a fabulous career as an experimental writer, capping it with a tenured position at Stanford University, not a shabby outcome for a guy who never graduated from college. But Sorrentino's literary knowledge was vast, even encyclopedic, and he deserved such honors.

If one looks at a magazine like Yugen, one sees all the writers' names who later became important figures in American poetry, including John Ashbery and Frank O'Hara, the editors of the magazine Hettie Jones and Amiri Baraka, Robert Creeley and Charles Olson, Diane Di Prima and Denise Levertov, Paul Blackburn and Joel Oppenheimer. Besides Sorrentino, Joel Oppenheimer exerted an important influence upon Selby's writing style. Many of the rhythms and the quirky typography—using slashes (/) instead of apostrophes ('), for instance—in Selby's prose are directly taken from Oppenheimer's poetry. The two were even roommates for a while. In fact, the best way to address Selby's prose is to treat it like poetry, using the same criteria of the direct treatment of the object, the rhythm of experience, and no ideas but in things. Also that Poundian concept of poetry being news that stays news can also be useful ways to approach the totality of Selby's prose style, which does not resemble any other prose style ever constituted on the page.

In 2001, I moved to England, planning to absorb some of our language at its root. I thought I would be there maybe a year or two, but I wound up living there fifteen years. Besides my US passport, I held an Irish one too, and that allowed me to work more easily than an American might in the circumstances. Early on in my stay, Selby suggested I visit his publisher, which at the time was Marion Boyars. She had fought an intense court battle in the 1960s to get Last Exit published in the UK, and she eventually won, although it caused a great deal of stress and tension in her life. Marion was gone, but her daughter still ran the press. She had agreed to meet me, but when I showed up, she wasn't that thrilled by my visit.

"A lot of people claim to be good friends with Cubby Selby," she said, suggesting that I was some kind of impostor.

"I've known Cubby for over thirty years," I said.

"A lot of people say that."

Eventually I left. Cubby had gotten his German publisher to reissue my novel The Brooklyn Book of the Dead, and I think he thought he could get Marion Boyars to publish the novel in the UK. But the daughter was singularly uninterested in my work.

Towards the end of Selby's life, he was in London for an interview with him at the South Bank Theatre, about a thousand people in attendance. He came out on stage wearing a blue blazer with gold buttons, a pair of slacks and loafers, with a white shirt, looking very elegant, especially with his walking stick to steady his gait.

The interview was classic Selby, his talking about his influences and his beginnings, and also his love of movies and his years in Hollywood.

Before the event I had called his publisher again because he wanted me to hook up with them and go to dinner after the event. Once again the daughter of Marion Boyars mentioned how a lot of people claimed to know Selby and unless she heard directly from him, she was not going to invite me to the dinner afterwards.

After the event on the South Bank, hundreds of people milled around, shaking the author's hand, telling him how much his writing meant to them. I inched my way forward to say hello to my old friend. In this sea of faces, Cubby looked up and spotted me, a fellow Brooklynite. "Mike," he shouted over the crowd, pointing to me, "yo, Mikey, get over here," he shouted in his thick Brooklyn accent. "Cubby!" I shouted back.

He let out his trademark maniacal laugh.

ANTS

by G. Murray Thomas

THINK OF an ant. A single ant crawling across your kitchen counter. No doubt on a search for food, following a trail only he can smell. When he finds a good patch, he will surely return to his anthill and bring the troops. Then you will have a line of ants, marching single file across your counter to the food source, and another line marching back with bits of food in their mandibles.

At that point, the ants are acting as a single entity, or, as ant expert Edward O. Wilson refers to it, a "superorganism." A group consciousness takes over; each ant acts not on its own decisions, but on direction from the colony.

But what about that individual ant in the first case? Is it out there on its own? It would seem so; its actions are determined by what it

finds – scent trails and such – and not by the group mind. At what point does it shift to being directed by the group? And is it aware of that shift?

I have become fascinated by this question – how does an individual entity become part of a group, to the point where it is subsumed in the group, where it loses its own identity to become part of a larger individual? How do separate entities become joined into a larger entity? Single cells unite and become multi-celled organisms. Bees develop a "hive mind" (a phrase which has entered our vocabulary in other contexts, which will be relevant shortly). Fish become schools, birds become flocks, wolves become packs. And what are the implications of all this for humanity?

Of course, each of these examples entails a different level of giving up the individual identity. A wolf can become a "lone wolf," but none of the cells in your body would survive on its own. You probably don't even think of those cells as being individuals, but they were once. You do probably think of starlings and guppies as individuals, but if you watch a flock of birds fly or a school of fish swim, they definitely appear to act as a single unit. Have you ever seen a mid-air collision in a flock in full flight? I never have.

Then there's the Portuguese Man'O'War. Just a big jellyfish, right? In fact, it is a siphonophore, a colony of separate creatures living together in a symbiotic relationship. These organisms function as organs, some as digestive, some as defensive, some as reproductive, while maintaining their individuality. Quite a concept, huh? So it exists somewhere between the single celled creatures, and full organisms like ourselves.

At the other extreme, we have the Gaia Hypothesis, which states that the earth, as a whole, functions as a single organism. All life is unified into a single living, breathing entity. The forests are the lungs, the oceans the digestive system, and the brain? We humans of course.

Looked at one way, we are hard-wiring that brain right now. What is the internet but a global brain? Which brings us back to that phrase, "hive mind." We use it all the time to refer to the group intelligence of the internet. The implication is that the internet is, or soon will be, a global consciousness.

If that's so, what role do individual humans play in that group mind? Where do individual humans fit in the overall social order?

Most of us think we are wolves. Yes, members of a pack, but fully capable of thinking for ourselves, of being that lone wolf. But in fact, few of us are. Not only incapable of surviving on our own, but we are often unable to think for ourselves without the directions of the pack. We may actually be more like that Man'O'War; we each have our role in the larger society, but very few of us could survive without the larger society around us. We are in the very definition of a symbiotic relationship with the other humans around us.

But the question here is, are we becoming like bees and ants, thinking with a group mind, losing our individuality? Where do we really stand, as we write our e-mails, post our pictures, share our memes? Enter our data, research our papers, buy our Christmas presents?

We think we are the ant following our own scent trail. But are we really just one in that long column of ants, following directions from a consciousness larger than ourselves? And if we are, would we even know?

Lady w/ tree - by Norman J. Olson

ART NOTES
AS REGARDS
NORMAN
OLSON

by Bill Tremblay

Four directions,
four winds,
four pictures stacked 2 x 2,
western prom-queen with one Mickey Mouse
   ear floating off like the balloon it is,

a picture of what the heart is like,
some thorns,
a lovely tree,
possibly fruit tree,
to the four-eyed angel fanning out her wings

like an angel with an older man in her,
it turns fuzzy like a Tarot card,
and the eponymous "Sequoia Tree" or its sign
    and symbol of a tree and its distant cousin,
both of which are still full of life.

The natural world lives on.

I have cartoons in my head. Sometimes I tell Cynthia about them, but it's always bloated billionaires burping hogwash like it's normal to be so piggish.

You travel and you take impressions. A woman in a triptych mirror. Who was "of three minds/like a tree with three blackbirds in it." Only in this case it's four. It works as a concatenation. Different radiances. However split

Sequoia Tree - by Norman J. Olson

The Guitar Player - by Norman J. Olson

the woman is slick magazine model of mature pulchritude. And yet the spines, the stuff that sticks out in the night, is right beside her and she's under-girded by a healthy tree in winter and this art deco figure all planes and curves and aforesaid radiance. Do not want to get cli-ched in some Freudian way into a bumbling in-terpretation of the womb area. Sickness/health; desert/mountain forest. Out of the cognitive dissonance comes a picture--divided energy and coherent energy. Divide, recombine in more interactive ways.

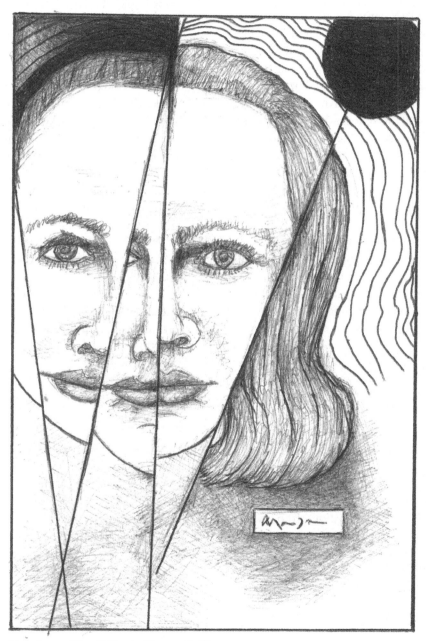

Four faces of Eve 1966 - by Norman J. Olson

REVIEWS

The Blues Drink Your Dreams Away
Selected Poems (1983 – 2018)

by John Macker

ISBN 9781946642745; Stuborn Mule Press
96 pages; $15

Review by RD Armstrong

WHEN JOHN contacted me about reviewing his new book, I had a hard time getting started. See, I've known John for twenty years, at least, and I hold him in high regard. Naturally, I wanted to do right by the guy.

John Macker, the man, lives in New Mexico. The terrain of the state lends itself to the use of image and metaphor when approaching the artistic expression of nature. There is an unstated air of the holy, if one is so inclined to see such things. I think most of the poetry I have seen/heard from this region draws inspiration from nature.

John Macker, the poet, interweaves image and metaphor in a tapestry which we call poem. For example this: "*Today, the universe exists at about eye level: a mound of green cedar, the December air, Raul and I in a sea-*

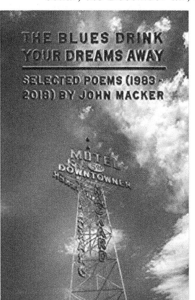

sonal exchange of trucks, wood and weather....perfect fuel for the dead of winter"(from Winter Solstice). Macker pulls his influences together, shakes them like runes in a cup and spills them in random configurations from which he draws the days work.

There are 92 poems in the collection. Of them, I have selected six poems for this review. I've chosen these six mainly because they are good examples of his style. The titles are: *A Day in the Life of an Altar Boy; No Exit Sutra; Beyond Geography; The Blues Drink Your Blues Away; Winter Solstice* and *Japanese Volcano*. These are the ones that struck me the most, that raised hairs or made me feel something. Not buzz words per se, but phrases that make this reader to go hmmm.

The thing I like in all poetry is a well-crafted line, one that catches me up and pricks that nerve in the back of my neck, the one that is attached to every "aha" I've ever had, and friends, Mr. Macker has that in spades! In **A Day in the Life of an Altar Boy**, he starts with a vivid image that is almost universal and moves into a memory that morphs into his "favorite things", his totems, if you will.

> I'm out in the churning wind of New Mexico,
> a cup of breakfast tea trembling in
> my hand, the latest war of the new
> century casts its underworld glow across
> the frozen tarn.
>
> I want to tell God's mirror
> I haven't been a Catholic for years
> but I believe in
> Apache arrowheads,
> hiking across soaring mountain
> streams, Joe Strummer & The Clash,
> the changing seasons of work & peace,
> solstice dusks with two good dogs,
> a life lived softly on the edge
> bereft of rancor,
> Elegaic Feelings American
> a desert river.

Consider "a life lived softly on the edge." Could this be a longing or a statement of fact? These last twelve lines could be a list of dreams or a recalling of events (macro or micro). I believe it was Gerry Locklin who once said that Bukowski could write about small things, making them larger than life. To my way of thinking this is part of Macker's craft, as well.

John Macker is an impressionist. His poetry paints a picture, which at first glance seems ordinary, but is in reality (well, at least in his reality) not so easily defined. In the desert, what appears to be harsh is often accompanied by intense beauty. You just have to wait for it...

As in these seven lines from the **No Exit Sutra**:

> The whistling breeze shakes the
> gold leaves loose,
> the pinyon jays
> shriek like
> renegrade
> witches
> of jazz.

"Pinyon jays shriek like renegade witches of jazz"; say what? That image makes my hairs stand up on the back of my neck, a sure sign that something's amiss, that day-dreaming stops here and the serious shit begins NOW. This image, tho cloaked in violence, also grabs the reader by the lapels and shakes them hard, trying to shock them and make them think. As to what they draw from this is up to them . We all draw from our experiences to help us understand what is happening.

I can almost see this as a scene in one of those surreal, Sergio Leone spaghetti westerns.... from **Beyond Geography**:

> we are this open work
> between words
> just a pair of stone desert
> exccentrics
> sipping cervezas,

> chatting up Borges, the
> blind Argentinian
> underneath the imaginary virga

Macker uses this imagery to 'paint' a scene, not only from his experiences but from his imagination.

Or this from **The Blues Drink Your Blues Away** (the title poem) which is dedicated to Tony Scibella*:

> surrogate mother of a morning
> the dawn is a suttee,
> a chaos pyre,
> the clouds are an armada of
> fossil scorpians;
> her beauty is this deep
> as the desert drags a
> dry razor
> across her face;

There are so many images in this poem that one might become overwhelmed or bored. Again if one loses focus, one loses the world! I am humbled.

Or consider this excerpt from **Winter Solstice**:

> For last night's full eclipse the blackened
> the earth, and dawn's
> slow exhalation of light
> I toss a log,
> and for this
> morning, startling a red-tailed hawk trying to
> get at the chipping sparrows hidden in
> the firethorn: to them
> the universe, a sanctuary,
> the giving thing.
> I toss a log.

Tony Scibella, an American poet and painter, who honed his craft in Venice, California (during the time of the Venice beats in the 60's) and later in Denver, Colorado until his death in 2003. He was 71. Scibella ran with two other poets who had been dubbed The Holy Three: Frank T. Rios and Stuart Z. Perkov.

The firewood here, becomes a metaphorical prayer, each log tossed into the fire becomes an offering, similar to lighting a candle for someone who is in trouble or has passed on. Macker expands this idea to include objects, animals and the desert.... all characters in his southwestern tableau. There is a hushed quality to this collection, and clearly Macker tips his hat to all things, spiritual or otherwise.

Finally, in the poem, **Japanese Volcano**:

Late snow flutters down
each flake
a flower petal
a performance
adrift......

still fluttering now
only more so
with the solemnity
of ash

These simple phrases paint a picture that become part of the legacy of the New Mexican poetry. This may not be Macker's intention, but as most poets know, once you put your work out there, you have no control over what happens to it. Poetry by nature relies on interpretation. Without it, stupid takes over.

Buy this book...before stupid takes over!

Café Crazy by Francine Witte
Kelsay Books, Aldrich Press,
www.kelsaybooks.com, 2018
Trade Paperback, 76pp. 2018. $14.00

Review by Linda Lerner

THE "HURT girls" from the title poem ("Café Crazy") is the author's persona, just as Charlie, in a series of Charlie poems, is a composite of various men they get involved with in their search for love. ("Other Charlies") Nor does she offer any solution to what often ends up being a cat and mouse game doomed to failure from the start. Admitting that she sometimes tells "the truths that didn't happen" to a pretend son, belies the intimate, confessional tone of these marvelous poems.

From the uncertainty of love, the poet considers how little we know about what's out there in the universe and just go along "futurestupid," worrying about little things instead, like "fashion and baseball and God knows what." ("By the Time I'm Born.")

In "There was a Time," Witte continues with this theme, considering a time when people believed the earth was flat, and that, "If you travelled far enough, / you'd simply fall off..." "to when love sometimes just goes flat; just as scientists disproved the flat earth theory, so a

Winner of the 2nd Annual Angela Mankiewicz Poetry Prize

NANCY SHIFFRIN

silly argument, doesn't prove "Love itself (has gone) flat."

By combining words Witte is able to encapsulate shades of meaning from a single thought. In "Stormbrew" she describes how "Cloudbruise/ and windwhisper (are) building" when a wife wakes up alone after her husband told her that he was leaving— "disasterscape of splinters and shards…and the slowmoving smoke of / heartbreak…"

In "Selfie at the End of the World" the obsession with photographing everything will even include the apocalypse she mockingly foresees; someone will "photobomb the last TV reporter, (with) humanity trampling / itself in the background."

What grabbed me immediately on reading the first few poems is the sharpness of Witte's language, her use of extending a metaphor to transition from where a poem begins to what it's really about. One of many examples is how she goes from a literal fire to "the fire of (her) husband and the other woman" she couldn't just "reason… away." And, when he limped back and kissed her, "she could taste the ashes still in his mouth." ("Not All Fires Burn the Same")

Witte also uses light like fire. It's the first command that God gave; what shows her skill is how she transitions from light…flooding the universe… to "that debut of stars" which would enable astronauts "eons later" to see as they walk in space, to the light in somebody's eyes when they say they love you. ("Overall Light")

That perennial "other woman" hovering about, is sniffed out when she's doing something like buying groceries. Still, she can't stop "loving a no-good man," walk away, or admit to needing more than "a carton of milk." ("Convenience") But, when it's over, there's always "that shade of faint regret that the once-loved always wears."

Café Crazy

Poems by Francine Witte

("Mother-in-Law") The recurrent figure is both a real woman and what keeps her man from making a commitment and reciprocating her love.

The Charlie figure toys with her, says, "give me your heart" and when she does, says, "it is mine now, / and later, I might / want it." ("Charlie Says Give Me Your Heart") He plays with love like an actor trying on different parts, gets down on his knees to propose as in an old movie. She doesn't buy what "looks like a man tying his shoe" and says, "get up." ("One Night, Charlie") In another poem he poses like "jimmy Dean." She sees the boy in his face. What begins as something casual, without her having to be "anyone's forever," he's gone and she doesn't know if she's coming or going. ("When Charley Goes James Dean on Me")

Sometimes, though less frequently in this collection, it's she, the woman, who gets bored, imagining how her life will be reduced to things like shopping and laundry and she'll be diminished like her mother was after her marriage. In "Years Later" we see her mother speaking up in the Bakery to get exactly what she wants; as she leaves, her daughter watches "her already starting to shrink" as she heads home.

Another theme in this collection is time; she wants the future back which hasn't come yet to her younger self and feels her life slipping out from under her. The past, present and future coalesce when she writes, "She's who I'm gonna be / ten years ago," and here we can only marvel at how much is packed into that phrase. ("Story of My Life")

Time passes. Everyone is getting older. Charlie is no longer young, and tries to regain his youth by flirting with the waitress as they're having dinner. "Your boybrain / still tricks you into thinking you could fuck the waitress if it weren't for me." ("Poem Where Charlie Gets It in the Gut") She and Charlie are friends now; she checks his status, and jokes, "there's plenty / like him out there in the sea." She wants to believe what she knows isn't true. ("Status") He leaves her in a swamp. She's patient. Charlie could return.

There's death too, now, which must be faced: her sister's which she's trying to come to terms with. Though both know it's inevitable, there's no harm in toying with it a bit: "to treat death like it's a boy/ we know will call, but it might be good / to play a little hard to get. ("My Sister is Dying")

While Witte doesn't find any joyous outcome where love is concerned, readers will enjoy following her on this metaphoric trek, and maybe, just maybe, will smile as they glimpse something of themselves reflected back.

Go out and get this book. You won't regret it.

New Found Land by Carolyn Clark

ISBN 9781681111957
Trade paperback, 78 pp.
$16.00 USD
(Cayuga Lake Books)

Review by Thelma T. Reyna, Ph.D.
Chief Editor/Publisher, Golden Foothills Press

IF I knew nothing of Dr. Carolyn Clark except her fourth book, New Found Land, I would quickly feel at home as with an old friend. The book lays bare her soul, and I admire what I see: immense devotion to all the elements that make life worth living: family, friends, mother earth with all its flora, fauna, infinite waters and heavens; an indefatigable love of seasons and the resilience they evoke and nurture; the landscapes of memory with their laser-like examination of unconditional love and unavoidable loss; a comfortable rapport with classical literature alongside an athleticism proving that the proverbial brain and brawn duality is still worthy of awe. This book is a portfolio of Clark's humanity, with her artistic gifts on full display in each of the 43 poems comprising this poetic gem.

Clark offers us glimpses of nature with painting-like descriptions, as in the title poem detailing Greenland on a long flight: "ocean tundra,/ fissures of olive hued rock/ reaped by glacial harrowing, labyrinths of fjords, dark blue,/ surfacing as snowmelt unzips new land." Whether with landscapes or animal life, Clark's powers of observation snap our eyes open to catch tiny details that delight, such as in "Hawk's Vision: I'm Winter," when Clark writes: "the dawn sun opened one eyelid,/ spilling Sicilian oranges/ through moon-soaked woods." Domesticated animals catch Clark's fancy, too: "a pig and a dog/ on the lee side of the ditch/ shared tangled cover in the naked berries," she reports in "Porch Wood." No detail of the natural world is unworthy of her notice, or

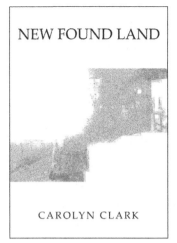

NEW FOUND LAND

CAROLYN CLARK

of her masterful appreciation and depiction of them.

Regarding people, Clark singles out a few defining traits, endearing acts, or memorable words and, in compact, economic strokes, she creates human beings who teach us a thing or two. The most profound of emotions—remembering a deceased father—takes on greater dignity in simplicity. In "Remembering to forget: choosing Lethe," Clark reminisces about her father's voracious reading and archiving of endless articles, stationed in the family's living room, his large desk facing the sidewalk and flanked by books of all genres and sizes. By aiming her poetic camera at two scenes simply described—her dad in their family home and then in a convalescent home in his frail years—Clark weaves threads of parallel similarities to cohere the two eras of her father's life: his love of reading , a comfortable chair, notations marking his place in his beloved books, a seeming detachment belying an unbreakable bond to his loved ones…or, as the poem states: "Perfect Love."

Other poems reveal the balance that running brings to life ("Crescent Trail Poem" and "Young Woman Jogger"), again an opportunity for Clark to depict nature brilliantly, and to reflect on the frailty of life. Others are paeans to romantic love, as is "Replenish: a birthday poem for Geoff." Or an homage to a sister ("Setting the Clock Ahead"). Whatever matters to Clark in this "our little palm of earth," as she says in her book's dedication page--such thoughts and values find themselves voiced elegantly in this book, much to the enrichment and contentment of our collective souls!

Fairfax and Other Poems
by David Del Bourgo
Quest Publishing Company 1985

Review by Nancy Shiffrin

"ALTHOUGH NOT religious," I won't work today," writes David Del Bourgo in his poem, "Yom Kippur". He is struggling to place himself vis-a-vis in his Jewish heritage. He will, however, eat on this fasting holy day, and listen to Mozart's Requiem Mass. A quiet irony in the selection of details is only one of Del Bourgo's strengths.

Del Bourgo is a moving and accessible poet. Another of his themes, conjugal relationship, is expressed in the poem "Magic". Walking late last night to give his wife (ex-wife?) money, another woman appears out of the darkness. He can see that she is possessed, "her/ nose some vague/ grammatical symbol printed on her face by a/drunken craftsman". In this poem, a contrast in styles pinpoints the failure of the marriage; i.e., the dramatic and mysterious language describing the unknown woman, the banal language describing the interaction with his wife, "we/spoke of how well & how poorly/we were doing apart.

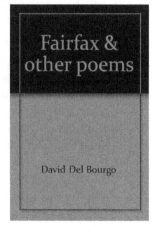

Del Bougo has a number of poems dedicated to composers. "Satie" best expresses what the poet himself is after in language, "a melody to make you weep/secretly…/the voice in the ear/& the exquisite fear of losing it."

I wrote this review in the mid-1980's for now a now defunct publication. It surfaced recently as I curate a life's work which I hope to publish as *Prose on Poets and Poetry*. Del Bourgo is a mature poet who was sure of his voice then and remains so. He still has books available.

Flow by Robin Scofield
(Street of Trees Project, 2017)

Review by Donna Snyder

ROBIN SCOFIELD writes in neat columns on the ruled pages of her blank books. I have seen those tidy lines when I sit next to her as she writes at Tumblewords Project, where we write on the spot and then read aloud what we just wrote. The lines travel down the page as if dictated by a divine and inerrant entity, seeming to appear fully formed and perfect on the blank page.

Divine and inerrant or not, I have heard Robin speak of significant revisions to her work. I have read published poems she wrote at Tumblewords Project's weekly workshops, which she has attended on a frequent basis since I founded it in 1995, and I have seen evident changes in work I had thought perfect as written on the blank page. Indeed, the digital version of *Flow* provided me for purposes of this review indicates in the document title that there were 23 previous versions of this book. Robin rules her muse with a hand both light and firm. She makes use of her keen editorial eye as the poetry editor for BorderSenses literary magazine.

Robin's first book, *Sunflower Cantos*, was described by Jennifer Clement, founder of the San Miguel Poetry Week and author of *Prayers for the Stolen*, as feeling "like an ecstatic channeling . . . [of] stunning, mysterious poems." The collection is from Mouthfeel Press as is Robin's earlier chapbook, *And the Ass Saw the Angel*. In *Sunflower Cantos*, we find a new mythology for modern times, expressed through the words of her creation, Cantalilly, who Robin has described as "a trickster goddess," and "a liminal figure both very much of the present as well as of the time before time." Here is a poem from *Sunflower Cantos*, "Driving, Cantalilly Finds Her Shroud."

and makes it a shield
on Doniphan Boulevard where they sell
the recently antique, collect impossible bones
and steel abs of muscle cars

lucky gas stations line up
to sell the winning broadside
for fields of clover figured in chaos

her shield is shrill white lace
figured in 1920's
warp and woof, treadle and song

she can see right through it

Flow, Robin's third collection of poetry, comprises poems that reflect what I have come to see as her major themes: chaos and flow theory, particle physics, family, and all things in the natural world, particularly the Chihuahua Desert of the West Texas/Northern Chihuahua/Southern New Mexico borderlands. Robin is intimately familiar with the flora and fauna she encounters on her lengthy daily walks with her dog, Winston, as well as on her frequent camping and hiking trips. *Flow*'s "Longing for Water" captures this understanding of her adopted homeland, as experienced by a mind schooled in the sciences.

Native bees dance in Brownian
motion around room-sized boulders
at Dripping Springs in the Organ
Mountains by the waterfall, a drip

more meek since there's been
no rain to speak of. The rock-ribbed
tortoise may be ancient, living on
gourmet horseflies in the damp cleft.

The summer's blue carapace stays in place
though dimensions outcrop like artichokes.
The steel-blue mountain jay lets drop
a dry stick, steals away in silence.

After demonstrating a predilection for poetry in her childhood, I understand that Robin pursued it scholastically, studying with acclaimed writers Albert Goldbarth, David Wevill, and Richard Howard. Since earning her degrees at the University of Texas in Austin, she has lived in El Paso, Texas for the past thirty years, teaching all manner of college classes, spanning the gamut of basic writing, mathematics in Spanish, general western civilization, and the Rhetoric of the Holocaust.

One hundred years ago, Dr. Frank Crane wrote an essay called "Tendency and Talent," found in Volume 9 of his collected works, Four Minute Essays (Wm. H. Wise & Co., Inc.: New York-Chicago, 1919). In it, Dr. Crane stated, "There is only one test [to distinguish a mere tendency from true talent]; talent carries with it the willingness to do any amount of hard work." By this standard, among others, Robin has talent by the gross. She has spent her life writing poetry, but also doing the work of reading voluminously. She has read and internalized the works of the literary canon, along with the mythology and the social and political history those writings represent. Moreover, she has read the great literature of many cultures, not merely the EuroAmerican masterpieces, but those originating in Asia, India, Latin America, and the magnificent societies of the eastern Mediterranean and Africa. In addition to the interest and tenacity to seek out culture throughout the world, Robin has also devoted substantial time to reading and learning about the principles of physics, cosmology, and mathematics.

Robin is a master gardener, with a special interest in native vegetation and xeriscaping, which is frequently evidenced in her poems. Here is "Desert Gardening: Esperanza," from *Flow*.

> Your seed is rather less prolific
> than we thought this winter
> that strips your ochre stems bare;
> like the words of an ancient language
> which drops out of the books whose pages crumble.
> Then you awaken past hope, yellow bells,
> trumpet flowers in the dry spring, late-comer.
> Flor de San Pedro,
> the white egrets shelter by boulders
> and choose wetlands full of reeds.
> I look up your names in the library
> of erosion. How, Tecoma Stans, is it
> that water catalogues all options at once?

And here, "Advent," also from *Flow*.

> Ravens are black plums
> that plummet over waxing pomegranate trees.
> Cottonwoods quilt the valley yellow,
> days dying early, so people feel trapped;
> they can't drive over crowded bridges
> to burnished grapevines
> throwing sparks at sunset.
> The dark comes on like a gullywasher.
> We're three weeks short of when the sun
> turns and the creamy light pours
> back a little at a time.
> I feel repentant,
> St. John chaining the angels.
> But it's early yet.

What bits of Robin Scofield's life are known to me, I have gleaned from biographical notes accompanying her publications, the occasional friendly conversation, and listening to her read at the weekly writing workshops of the Tumblewords. Although born in Austin, Texas, Robin grew up just north of Dallas, reading poems from her parents' *New Yorker Magazine* and riding horses. Her extended family of intellectuals, artists, lawyers, and judges immersed her in erudition and the arts, as well as the always topical issues of civil rights, egalitarianism, racism, sexism, and mental illness. All of these issues, whether directly or indirectly, reveal themselves in Robin's poetry, including her most recent collection, Flow, released in 2017 by Street of Trees Project. A three-page prose poem in *Flow*, "Field Medicine," details some of the salient details of the Scofield family. It begins, "My father was born in a sawmill in Zerath,/a possibly mythical place in deep east Texas,/in the Big Thicket where rare woodpeckers knock…." Of her parents, she says, "…They made a dashing couple in the 50s & 60s, jazz-age wannabes, hard drinkers and fast drivers." Robin's father was a civil rights advocate, a lawyer, and at some point in his life, a judge. Her mother was a brainy eccentric. In another poem, "Revelation," she revisits her childhood.

It rains for seven days around
my sister's fourth birthday
when she stabs her coloring
books grackle-black, and I sit
sentinel in the hackberry tree.
At seven, I know some things:
that grease flames are dark,
that orange rhymes with red,
that black spiders bite,
that you can't drive a nail
through knotty wood,
that Mother grabs a knife
and chases me, that there are doors
I can't walk through
though something galloping
in my head can.
My mother screams
in her sailor's tongue,
and her mouth shrivels
as if she bites into
a green persimmon

while she flies
out the back door,
the skillet a tower
of black smoke,
her curse an O
as the swallows
fall into sunset.

Flow's title can be seen as relating to the psychological theory popularized in the 1970s Hungarian-American psychologist, Mihály Csikszentmihály, involving a person's complete immersion in work or a project, often thought of in terms of artists or scientists who are challenged by their work while also being highly adept. Observing Robin write at Tumblewords Project workshops illustrates flow theory quite well. She becomes completely absorbed as the words and images appear on the paper before her in a seemingly effortless manner. Flow is also described as applying to musical performance, such as improvisational musicians and hip hop artists when they hit their groove and nothing exists for them at that moment but the notes or words spinning out from their individual creative genius, apt comparisons to Robin in the act of creation. Likely an autotelic personality, which I understand to be a person who does something for its own sake rather than to achieve an external goal, Robin demonstrates what Nicola Baumann described in 2012 as involving both openness, engagement, and persistence, that is, both a psychological trait and an aspect of execution. When writing, Robin appears to take whatever random stimulation from her immediate environment and transform it into a work of art, while completely immersed in the process, as opposed to intellectually contriving an end goal and then pursuing it.

The term "flow" is also used in physics and applies to what is called the Constructal Law as described by Adrian Bejan, a professor of Mechanical Engineering at Duke University. In an interview published in *Forbes* Magazine in February of 2012, Bejan is interviewed by Anthony Wing Kosner. According to Professor Bejan, "The Constructal Law is . . . a universal tendency . . . toward design in nature, in the physics of everything. This tendency occurs because all of nature is composed of flow systems that change and evolve their configurations over time so that they flow more easily, to create greater access to the currents they move." All of nature is inherently patterned in repeating designs at a micro and macro level. Robin's collection of poetry also reflects these patterns, frequently dealing with bodies of water, or water's lack, and other themes occurring and reoccurring throughout the book. Consider the poem "Speech Gesture."

> Why is the wind inside the spiral shell
> twisting code into the echo of my ear,
> a white noise like the highway tides
> I decipher? The Gila River unravels
> an ancient sea. The stars announce
> their names, whose light leaves earlier
> than leaves fall, and fall is a point
> in orbit whose campfire pages roll
> print onto near faces, the ocean in
> the veins broken blue by winter cold
> that's coming in a wave of sunset
> lighter than the shade of my blood
> in which a boat rises when I hear
> her reading Rilke in her native German.

Robin Scofield's book is well named as both the poet and the poems in it epitomize the diverse theories of flow, a law, not a theory, that can be seen as applying to everything from the design of leaves to the natural pattern of rivers. Its organizational principles are found in fractals and snowflakes, as well as the writing and performance of poetry. Flow is an excellent book and I recommend it to anyone who is interested in the topography of the Southwestern United States or the application of scientific theory in the writing of poetry.

CONTRIBUTORS

Austin Alexis is the author of *Privacy Issues* (Broadside Lotus Press, 2014), which received the Naomi Long Madgett Poetry Award for a first full-length collection. He is also the author of two previously published chapbooks from Poets Wear Prada. His work has appeared in *Barrow Street, The Journal, The Pedestal Magazine* and elsewhere, and he has work forthcoming in *Poets to Come: A Whitman Bicentennial Anthology*. He has received scholarships from the Bread Loaf Writers' Conference and the Vermont Studio Center.

RD Armstrong has had a haphazard career in poetry...first he was a poet, then he became a small (some would say micro) press publisher. Then he was a poet/publisher, then a publisher who dabbled in poetry. Now he's trying to resurect his "career" as a poet (while struggling with early onset Dementia). His new book, *Orphaned Words*, has been getting solid reviews; LUMMOX Press is becoming a respected poetry publisher...who knows, he might even be able to make a spartan living from all this afterall! Time will tell. *www.lummoxpress.com*

Belinda Berry developed a life-long love of travel and community advocacy and as an avid reader since childhood, she has aspired to become a better writer for most of her life. Belinda has earned degrees from UC Santa Barbara and the University of La Verne, raised four children, and recently retired from teaching middle school English. While continuing to work with students outside the classroom tutoring and facilitating a poetry performance, she is following her passion for writing through workshops and exploring meaningful life events through poetry and memoirs.

Jay Blommer is a visionary visual artist/poet who uses a multi-media approach to his themes which he then delivers to the public using redacted ironic messages adding a wry nudge-nudge, wink-wink of political savvy to the 'converstation'. He also has a family and holds down a job. He's golden!

Chris Bodor left his New York City job of ten years and moved to Saint Augustine, Florida in the summer of 2003. With a book of dog eared poems in hand, he turned on a microphone at a coffee shop in August of 2009 and invited the community to sign up and share words or just listen. Everyone who reads at the open mic is known as an "Ancient City Poet". They still gather on the last Sunday of the month, to this day.

Brenton Booth lives in Sydney, Australia. His latest collection *Bash the Keys Until They Scream* is available form Epic Rites Press.

Lynn Bronstein is the author of four poetry collections, *Astray from Normalcy, Roughage, Thirsty in the Ocean,* and *Border Crossings*. Her poetry and short fiction have been published in *Playgirl, Beyond Baroque*

Obras, California State Poetry Quarterly, Poetry Superhighway, poeticdiversity, Silver Birch Press, Chiron Review, Galway Review, LUMMOX, Spectrum, and *Voices from Leimert Park*, among others. She has been a journalist for five decades, writing for the *Los Angeles Times* and other Los Angeles area newspapers. She has been nominated for two Pushcart Prizes for poetry and for two Best of the Net Awards for short fiction.

Heath Brougher is the poetry editor of *Into the Void*, winner of the 2017 and 2018 Saboteur Awards for Best Magazine. He has published 8 collections of poetry, the most recent being *The Ethnosphere's Duality* (Cyberwit, 2018) and *Tangential Dithyrambs* (Concrete Mist Press, 2019). He is a multiple Pushcart Prize and Best of the Net Nominee as well as winner of the 2018 Poet of the Year Award from *Taj Mahal Review.*

Patricia Brown Ph.D. (Gayatri) is a clinical psychologist in New Mexico and president of *WisdomWave.org.* Severe community devastation propelled her creative expression, noted in *Artists of the Spirit.* From a 33-year apprenticeship with the now deceased Dr. Shrikrishna Kashyap, she authored his memoir as well as *The Little Book of the Self, The Supplicate Order,* journal articles, CDs, a children's book, and 2 musicals (*Ave* and *Mundo Tercero* in production). Obtaining grants for after-school arts, she also served on executive committees for a community theater an integrative medicine. Her painting appears in *The Mirrors of the Mind III: The Psychotherapist as Artist.*

B.J. Buckley is a Montana poet and writer who has worked in Arts-in-Schools/Communities programs throughout the west and midwest for over 37 years. She is currently SD Arts Council Writer-in-Residence for Sanford Arts, Sanford Cancer Center, Sioux Falls, SD. Her poems have appeared widely in small print and on-line journals, and she has received a number of national prizes and awards for her work. Her poetry books include *Moonhorses and the Red Bull,* with co-author Dawn Senior-Trask (Prong Horn Press 2005); a letterpress chapbook, *Spaces Both Infinite and Eternal* (Limberlost Press 2013); and *Corvidae* , with woodcut illustrations by Dawn Senior-Trask (LUMMOX Press 2014).

Wayne F. Burke has published six full-length poetry collections, most recently *DIFLUCAN* (BareBack Press, 2019). He lives in the State of Doubt, NW of Boston, S of Montreal, E of Sheecago (that wunnerful town).

Helmut Christoferus Calabrese was born in Germany; he immigrated to the United States in 1962. He began writing poetry and music after graduating high school in 1975. He earned a Ph.D. in music composition from New York University. His poems have been published in *Big Hammer* and *Street Value* (David Roskos, publisher) and *LUMMOX* (RD Armstrong, publisher). His music is published by Calabrese Brothers Music and distributed by the Subito Music Corporation. His first book of poetry, *New Creation: Collected Poems Of Helmut Christoferus Calabrese 1975 – 2019,* was published in 2019 by Iniquity Press/ Vendetta Books.

Calokie (Carl Stilman) is a humble country poet from Oklahoma who taught for nearly 35 years for Los Angeles City schools and now live in Pasadena.He has poems published in *Altadena Poetry Review, Blue Collar Review, Canary, LUMMOX, Pearl, Prism, Revolutionary Poets Brigade--Los Angeles, Spectrum*, and *Struggle.* He also has poems included in the anthologies, *an Eye For An Eye Makes The Whole World Blind/Poets On 911,* and *In the Arms of Words: Poems for Tsunami Relief..*

Don Kingfisher Campbell, MFA in Creative Writing from Antioch University Los Angeles, has taught a Writers Seminar at Occidental College Upward Bound for 35 years, been a coach and judge for *Poetry Out Loud*, a performing poet/teacher for Red Hen Press Youth Writing Workshops, Los Angeles Area Coordinator and Board Member of California Poets In The Schools, publisher of *Spectrum* and *the San Gabriel Valley Poetry Quarterly*, organizer of the *San Gabriel Valley Poetry Festival*, and host of the *Saturday Afternoon Poetry reading series* in Pasadena, California. For awards, features, and publication credits, please go to: *http://dkc1031.blogspot.com*

Alan Catlin has been publishing for better part of five decades. Among his many full length books and chapbooks are two LUMMOX titles: "Last Man Standing" and the Little Red Book, "Death and Transfiguration Cocktail. His most recent full length book is "Still Life with Lighthouse" from Cyber Wit. He is the poetry editor of the online poetry journal Misfit Magazine.

Chuka Susan Chesney, Susan Chesney, a graduate of Art Center College of Design, is an artist, poet, and editor. Her poems have been published on four continents. *You Were a Pie So We Ate You*, a book of Chesney's poems won the 2018 San Gabriel Valley Poetry Festival Chapbook Contest. In November 2018, Chesney hosted a poetry reading with Don Kingfisher Campbell for YEAR ONE exhibition featuring Loren Philip and Tomoaki Shibata's collaborative art at Castelli Art Space in Mid City. Chesney's anthology of poetry and art *Lottery Blues*, coedited by Ulrica Perkins will be published by Little Red Tree Publishing in 2019.

Jackie Chou is a poet residing in sunny Southern California. She likes to identify as a neurodivergent poet as she has battled bipolar disorder most of her adult life and writes about her experience with mental illness. She writes about other topics as well. She has been published in *LUMMOX, Altadena Poetry Review,*

JOMP 21 Dear Mr President anthology, *Creative Talents Unleashed* anthologies, and others.

Jonathan Church is an economist and writer.

Wanda Clevenger lives in Hettick, IL – population 200, give or take. Over 600 pieces of her work appear in 169 print and electronic publications. The first two volumes of a 5-volume set *where the hogs ate the cabbage* have published through Writing Knights Press: *young and unadorned*: *https://writingknightspress.blogspot. com/2017/12/young-and-unadorned-by-wanda-morrow.html* and *no dyeing in machines*: *https:// writingknightspress.blogspot.com/2018/12/no-dyeing-in-machines-by-wanda-morrow.html*

Sharyl Collin enjoys writing, reading, photography and music. Her poems have appeared in *Redondo Poet's 1001 Nights Anthology, LUMMOX, Switched on Gutenberg, * 82 Review* and *Wild Goose Poetry Review*. Sharyl lives in Lomita, California and usually has a guitar, notebook or camera in hand.

Beverly M. Collins is the Author of the books, *Quiet Observations: Diary thought, Whimsy and Rhyme* and *Mud in Magic*. She has appeared in *California Quarterly, Poetry Speaks! A year of Great Poems and Poets, The Hidden and the Divine Female Voices in Ireland, The Journal of Modern Poetry, Spectrum, The Altadena Poetry Review* and many others. In 2012, she won a prize from the California State Poetry Society. She was twice nominated for the Pushcart Prize(In 2015 & 2018) and once for Best Independent American Poetry, she was "short listed" for the 2018 Pangolin Review Poetry prize.

Patrick Conners' chapbook, *Scarborough Songs*, was published by Lyricalmyrical Press in 2013, and charted on the Toronto Poetry Map. *Part-Time Contemplative*, his second chapbook with Lyricalmyrical, was released in 2016. He has recently been accepted for publication by the Blue Collar Review, Harbinger Asylum, and *Tamaracks*, the first anthology of Canadian poets published in the USA in over 30 years. He is a manager of the Toronto chapter of 100,000 Poets for Change.

Blair Cooper lives in Santa Fe where she paints and writes poetry. She has published in various Southwestern journals, in *Sin Fronteras* frequently, and in *LUMMOX*. Currently, she's in the throes of publishing a collection of her poems amid frequent distractions.

Kit Courter is the causative element behind the books *"Shasta Cycle"* and *"California Trees"*, as well as other stuff (mostly self-published short-swimmer cases and a little evidence of lunatic photography). He hangs his hat on the lamp post at the border of Torrance and Redondo Beach, and as a consequence is pretty much a reformed aerospace engineer that hopes to revisit his hippy philosophy childhood.

Henry Crawford is a poet whose work has appeared in several journals and online publications including *Boulevard, Copper Nickel* and *The MetaWorker*. His first collection of poetry, *American Software*, was published in 2017 by CW Books. His poem *Blackout* was selected by the Southern Humanities Review as a finalist in the 2018 Jake Adam York Witness Poetry Contest. His multimedia poem, *Windows and Secrets* was a finalist in the 2018 Slippery Elm Journal Multimedia Poetry Contest. His website is HenryCrawfordPoetry.com.

William Craychee is a baby boomer. He had no control over when he was born or over the social and historical context in which he was born. He has been a witness to many changes: the end of a Cold War and the beginning of the Internet. The rise of globalism. The rise of populism. A few little poems are an apt distraction.

Sue Crisp writes in many different forms of poetry and has been published in *Medusa's*

Kitchen, NiceNet, Voices of Lincoln, Nature Writing, The Orchards, MoSt Poetry, The Avocet, LUMMOX Anthology 6 & 7, and others.

Ann Curran is the author of 2 chapbooks: *Placement Test* and *Irish Eyes* (both Main Street Rag) and 2 books: *Me First* for which she was nominated for a Pushcart Prize and *Knitting the Andy Warhol Bridge* (both LUMMOX Press), Her poetry has appeared in *Rosebud Magazine, U.S. 1 Worksheets, Off the Coast, Ireland of the Welcomes, Commonweal, LUMMOX Poetry Anthologies* and *The New York Times*, She lives in Pittsburgh, PA with husband Ed Wintermantel.

Poet/collagist **Steve Dalachinsky** was born in Brooklyn in 1946. His book *The Final Nite* (Ugly Duckling Presse - 2006) won the PEN Oakland National Book Award. His latest cds are *The Fallout of Dreams* with Dave Liebman and Richie Beirach (Roguart 2014), *ec(H) o-system* with the French art-rock group, the Snobs (Bambalam 2015) and *Pretty in the Morning with the Snobs* (Bisou Records – 2019). He is a 2014 recipient of a Chevalier D' le Ordre des Artes et Lettres. His newest book *where night and day become one – the french poems* (great weather for MEDIA, 2018) received a 2019 IBPA award in poetry.

Seven Dhar pushes the limits of language, East and West, performing in Sanskrit and Gaelic, Spanish and the awed tongue of mystics as a Buddhist yogi urban shaman with Native American L.A. roots; graduate of UC Berkeley and UCLA, who also studied at Yale and Oxford; winner of the SGVPF chapbook and broadside contests; voted "poet laureate" at Poetrypalooza 2016; host of the Askew Reading Series in Pasadena; published in *Coiled Serpent, Eagle Rock Library Anthology, Altadena Poetry Review, Yay! LA Magazine, The Border Crossed Us, Spectrum, LA Word Salon's LAWS Review, Heartbreak, Hometown-Pasadena*; featured poet at LitFest Pasadena, Poets in Distress.

CONTRIBUTORS

Helen Donahoe has always enjoyed reading. When she was old enough to walk the few blocks to the library, she began her sojourn as a reader. For years it was her favorite place. At thirteen she read The Count Of Monte Cristo and Jane Eyre. When the staff saw what she was reading they allowed her to stay in the adult section, at a table near their lobby desk. She started writing later in life and enjoyed it. Over the years she's written short stories, poems, and started two long mystery stories that she hopes to finish sometime soon.

Alicia Viguer-Espert is interested in the seen and the unseen, the mysterious quotidian events of body and spirit; she enjoys finding new pathways to express thoughts, feelings and perceptions. Much is foreign to her but she's a quick learner. *LUMMOX Anthology, Altadena Poetry Reviews, ZZyZx Intersections, Spectrum*, among other publications have been graced with her poems. Her book *Holding a Hummingbird* was the winner of 2017 San Gabriel Valley Poetry Festival Book Contest. She lives in Southern California with her husband and seven singing canaries.

Mark Evans is currently an expat residing in Portugal, and was a recent resident of Joshua Tree, CA (2017) by way of Wichita, KS. He has lived in various cities throughout California during nomadic, but formative, years—finally settling in Los Angeles. Mark had always been an aspiring writer of music and lyrics—but found a more expressive niche in poetry. He is the author of a notable poetry book: *Hotel Linen* [2015]. His latest collection of poetry, entitled: *The Dogs Behind the Fence*, was released in June 2018.

L.A. poet **Alexis Rhone Fancher** is published in *Best American Poetry, Verse Daily, Plume, The American Journal of Poetry, Rattle, Hobart, Diode, Nashville Review, Wide Awake, Poets of Los Angeles, The New York Times*, and elsewhere. She's the author of 5 poetry collections; *How I Lost My Virginity To Michael Cohen*, (2014), *State of Grace: The Joshua Elegies*, (2015), *Enter Here*, (2017), *Junkie Wife*, (2018), and *The Dead Kid Poems* (2019). *EROTIC, New & Selected*, publishes in 2020 from New York Quarterly. A multiple Pushcart Prize and Best of the Net nominee, Alexis is poetry editor of Cultural Weekly. *www. alexisrhonefancher.com*

Joseph Farley edited Axe Factory 186 - 2010. His books and chapbooks include *Suckers, For the Birds. Longing for the Mother Tongue*, and *Her Eyes*. A novel, *Labor Day*, will be coming out in a second edition from Peasantry Press. His work has appeared recently in *US 1 Worksheets, LUMMOX 7, Ygdrasil, Mad Swirl, Wilderness House Review*, and *Hone Planet News Online*.

Gwendolyn Fleischer is a SoCal native who enjoys all things creative. Age 8, she sold a poem to a friend for a quarter. Today, she is involved in several poetry groups. Gwendolyn enjoys performing original and cover songs on the guitar and keyboard, as well as acting and painting. She private teaches singing and piano to all age groups. You can usually find her riding her red motorbike. Gwendolyn also enjoys road trip adventures with her sweetie.

Dennis Formento, a poet and activist, lives in Slidell, LA, across Lake Pontchartrain from his native New Orleans. He is the author of *Spirit Vessels* (FootHills Publishing, 2018), *Cineplex* (Paper Press, 2014,) *Looking for An Out Place* (FootHills Publishing, 2010.) Edited *Mesechabe: The Journal of Surregionalism* and founded Surregional Press. Formento studied poetry at Naropa Institute and the University of Colorado. Since 2011 he has been organizing readings in New Orleans and in Covington, LA, for *100,000 Poets for Change*, a world-wide movement for peace, ecological sustainability, justice and cultural exchange.

Roseanna Frechette is simply in love with words. She considers it a high honor to be published by the fantastic small presses of the world. But truth be known~ Roseanna will always be happy to explore a writer's World of Words in any crossing-of-genres way that leads to blowing the mind open while also connecting with the very heart of humanity.

Bill Gainer is a storyteller, a humorist, an award winning poet, and a maker of mysterious things. He earned his BA from St. Mary's College and his MPA from the University of San Francisco. He is the publisher of the PEN Award winning R. L. Crow Publications and is the ongoing host of Red Alice's Poetry Emporium (Sacramento, CA). Gainer is internationally published and known across the country for giving legendary fun filled performances. His latest book is *The Mysterious Book of old Man Poems* (LUMMOX Press, 2018). Visit him in his books, at his personal appearances, or at his website: *billgainer.com.*

William Scott Galasso is the author of fifteen books of poetry including *Mixed Bag*, (A Travelogue in Four Forms), 2018, available on Amazon and was editor/contributing poet of *Eclipse Moon*, (2017), the 20th Anniversary issue of Southern California Haiku Study Group. His next collection *Rough Cut* is due out this summer. He's an award winning poet, who's had works magazines in more than 225 journals, anthologies and on-line magazines in more than fifteen countries worldwide. In addition, he's participated in 300 readings, appearing on TV and radio programs in Washington, New York, New Mexico and California. *It's not the words, it's how you use them.*

Martina R. Gallegos came from Mexico and attended Pasadena High school, Oxnard College, CSUN. She got a Master's from Grand Canyon University after a big stroke, coma, Achilles and heart surgeries. Her work's appeared in *Hometown Pasadena, Altadena Poetry Review:*

Anthology 2015, Latino Authors, LUMMOX, Central Coast Poetry Shows, Spirit Fire Review, Silver Birch Press, Poetry Super Highway, La Bloga, vocal.media, and *Basta!*

Matt Galleta lives in upstate New York. A collection of poems, *The Ship Is Sinking*, is available from Epic Rites Press. Find out more at *www.mattgalletta.com.*

Kathleen Goldman lives and writes in Manhattan Beach. When she isn't scrambling for the right word or the best line break—or where the comma belongs, she scrambles after her grandchildren and the dust bunnies the cats create each day. Her book, Down River, came out in 2014. She hopes to have another ready to submit for publication by the end of this year.

James Gould, a former secondhand bookseller, has been chasing a variety of art forms in northern New Mexico for over twenty years. He received an Honorable Mention for poetry in the 2018 SFCC Katie Besser Writing Awards, secured third place for fiction in the 2017 Santa Fe Reporter Writing Contest and is a participant in the Telepoem Booth project. His present creative inquiry and practice is centered within his workspace, *The Trapezium*, so named for its shape wherein no two surfaces are parallel.

Lorraine Gow has been an educator and a college writing coach. She's an immigrant from Honduras, and as such, many of her writings embrace the various cultures, religions and traditions of her family and people she has met along her life's journey. Ms. Gow's writings have appeared in the *Village Stories 2015, 2016 and 2017 Anthology, LUMMOX Poetry Anthology* and *Life and Legends Literary Journal*. She is currently working on a collection of short stories about the experiences of black immigrant women.

Kenneth Greenley is a writer and poet living and working in Denver, Colorado. The number of places he's lived is only exceeded by the number of jobs he's had. Greenley likes to explore the themes of class division (in a supposedly classless country), the struggle to stay spiritual in the modern world, and first-time experiences of any kind. The main mission of his writing is to make people laugh and think at the same time. His new book, *Back Alley Poems*, can be purchased on Amazon.com. He is the winner of the 2015 Gerald Locklin Award.

Friday Gretchen dwells in Ventura, [Calif.] where she helped to establish poet laureate & youth poet laureate posts within her county. She is an advocate for the arts: literary, visual & performance. She has performed her work internationally and has been published numerous times, most notably in *Art/Life, Askew, Miramar, Spillway* and within a handful of anthologies about birds. Her inaugural book of selected poems, *Unkindnesses*, will debut mid-2019 from Old Hat Press.

Tom Gannon Hamilton is founder/curator/host of the Toronto Urban Folk Art Salon; his poems have appeared in *Blue Buffalo, Blood & Aphorisms, Transforms, Hart House, Whetstone, Dalhousie reviews, Verse Afire, Delicate Impact, Banister anthologies* and *Artis magazine*. In 2018 Tom's poem suite El Marillo won 1st prize in the Big Pond Rumours chapbook contest; his book *Panoptic* (Aeolus House) was nominated for a Pushcart Prize as well as the Gerald Lampert Award.

Vijali Hamilton has for the past thirty-five years, worked and taught around the world as an artist-poet/peacemaker. She collaborates with diversified communities and utilizes her skills as a sculptor, filmmaker, poet, musician, and author. Vijali started her World Wheel Project in 1986 to further explore the role that community-based art can play in building a world at peace.

Charles Harmon first published a short story in the local newspaper in 4th grade, followed by hundreds of poems, stories, songs, articles, a novel, screenplays, and essays. He won a national science teaching award from the NSTA in 2001 and $20,000 for his "Don't Be a Crash Test Dummy!" project. He uses poetry to motivate students, challenging them to write their own. He reviewed, edited, and contributed to five textbooks for Houghton Mifflin. A world traveler, Charles has spent five years overseas and taught English as well. He was named a "Top Ten San Gabriel Valley Poet" by Spectrum.

Clarinda Harris, a professor emerita of Towson University, has recently published her 7th poetry collection, *INNUMERABLE MOONS* with art by Peter Bruun. She continues her multi-decade oversight of BrickHouse Books, Inc., MD's oldest literary press as well as teaching workshops at Pratt Library in Baltimore and working with prison writers.

Sarah Henry studied with two former U.S. Poet Laureates at the University of Virginia. She has published internationally in many journals, and recently in the anthology *300,000 Years of Us*. Sarah is retired from a newspaper and lives in a small Pennsylvania town without distractions.

Debra Okun Hill is a Canadian poet who gardens words full-time in rural southwestern Ontario. To date, over 415 of her poems have been published in publications/e-zines including *LUMMOX, TAMARACKS, Mobius, Still Point Arts Quarterly, The Binnacle, THEMA* and *Phati'tude Literary Magazine* in the United States. She has one trade book published by Black Moss Press and four award-winning chapbooks. She blogs about literary happenings including LUMMOX's Canadian launches at *http://okunhill.wordpress.com/*

Gil Hagen Hill is California native. He was born Culver City. He received a BA in Theater Arts from California State University, Los Angeles in 1973. He has worked as a professional actor, bartender, bouncer, cook,carpenter - sold sewer pipe, automobiles and motorcycles. He's been published in numerous poetry journals and anthologies - *Verses Magazine, Hazmat Literary review* - the various iterations of the *LUMMOX Journal* and *Last Call; The Legacy of Charles Bukowski* edited by RD Armstrong. His first Chap Book *"Circle of Bones"* from LUMMOX Press was nominated for a Pushcart award in 2018.

Lori Wall-Holloway lives in the San Gabriel Valley in California where her poetry appeared in the *San Gabriel Valley Poetry Quarterlies*. Her work has also been included in the *Altadena Poetry Review from 2015-2019, the Spectrum anthologies* and *LUMMOX 7.*

Alex Johnston lives and works in the Fingerlakes region of upstate New York. He's the author of the book *On Fire and Roses*, (LUMMOX Press, 2018). He is currently working on his second collection of poetry entitled, *Crocodile*. I have been writing poetry for roughly five years and hope to one day teach in a university.

Jackie Joice will be practicing her desert juju as a new resident of Corona, CA. She's a photographer, paper crafter, and writer on hiatus.

Frank Kearns is a transplanted New Englander and a longtime California resident. He is the author of two poetry collections, *"Circling Venice"* (2013) and *"Yearlings"* (2015). His work has also appeared in anthologies such as *"Beyond the Lyric Moment," "Like a Girl: Perspectives on Feminism," "The California Writers Club Literary Review," "Now and Then,"* and a number of editions of the *LUMMOX anthology.*

Lalo Kikiriki was born in Oklahoma, grew up in Texas; and moved to California in 1979, after ten years on Pacifica Radio Houston and publication of a chapbook, *Old Movies,*

Other Visions, with Pam Palmer. lalo earned a Masters Degree in Humanities from Cal State Dominguez Hills, 2007; she is also a ZZyZx Writer, itinerant accordionist, amd queen of Poetrypalooza 2015.

Diane Klammer is a poet, musician, songwriter, therapist and retired biology teacher. A California native, she now makes her home in Boulder Colorado. Her work has appeared widely internationally and online including Rattle, Open Earth from Pudding, Spaces, Iron Velo, Avocet, Fast Forward, LUMMOX and elsewhere. She currently has a blog where she archives poems, stories and songs called Diane Klammer Poetry, one book, Shooting the Moon and fodder for unfinished manuscripts. She is grateful people from wide backgrounds contribute to the art of poetry. She tries to approach her writing with a spirit of humor compassion and honestly.

Maureen Korp is a military brat, the daughter of an American soldier. She grew up in faraway places, including Okinawa, Hokkaido, Oklahoma, Texas, and Germany. Home base today is Ottawa, Canada. She is an independent scholar, writer, and art critic. Dr. Korp has lectured at universities throughout the United States and Canada, as well as eastern Europe (1995-2015) and Pakistan (2008-10) on the intertwined histories of art and religions. Her publications are numerous (more than 120 articles and three books), including a number of poems in little magazines and anthologies, most recently, Tamaracks, and LUMMOX #7.

Michou Landon is a minister of the invisible, a hapless wordsmith, last sighted in Santa Fe, New Mexico.

Donna Langevan's latest poetry collections include *The Laundress of Time*, (Aeolus House 2014) and *Brimming*, (Piquant Press, 2019). Short-listed for the **Descant 2010 Winston Collins prize**, she won second prize in the

GritLIT contest in 2014, and in the *Banister Anthology Competition 2017.* In 2014 and 2015, her plays, *the Dinner* and *Bargains in the New World* won first prizes for script at the Eden Mills Festival. *If Socrates Were in My Shoes* was produced at the Alumnae Theatre NIF Festival in 2018 and she is the co-author of *Waiting for Attila* which won a staged reading at NIF, 2019.

Laura Munoz-Larbig received a Bachelor's Degree in English from CSULB in 1980, Creative Writing Emphasis. Since 1977, her poetry and prose has appeared in college and private anthologies, plus editorials in local newspapers. Poems and two essays were published in *LUMMOX Number 2, 3, 4, 6,* and *7.* A poem in Vol 7, *Land of Smokes,* has been edited to appear in Psalms of Cinder & Silt, published by Solo Novo Press.

Hiram Larew's poems have appeared recently in *Voices of Israel, the New Oxford, Words for the Wild, Contemporary American Voices, The Wild Word* and elsewhere. His fourth collection, *Undone,* was issued in December 2018 from FootHills Publishing. Nominated for four Pushcarts, he's is a global hunger specialist, and lives in Upper Marlboro, MD. On Facebook at Hiram Larew, Poet, at *Poetry X Hunger* and at *The Poetry Poster Project.*

Kyle Laws is based out of the Arts Alliance Studios Community in Pueblo, CO where she directs Line/Circle: Women Poets in Performance. Her collections include *Ride the Pink Horse* (Stubborn Mule Press), *Faces of Fishing Creek* (Middle Creek Publishing), *So Bright to Blind* (Five Oaks Press), and *Wildwood* (LUMMOX Press). With six nominations for a Pushcart Prize, her poems and essays have appeared in magazines and anthologies in the U.S., U.K., Canada, and France. She is the editor and publisher of Casa de Cinco Hermanas Press.

Marie C. Lecrivain is the executive editor of *poeticdiversity: the litzine of Los Angeles,*

an associate editor for *Good Works Review,* a photographer, and a writer-in-residence at her apartment. Her work has appeared in various journals, including: *Gargoyle, The Los Angeles Review, Nonbinary Review, Orbis, Pirene's Fountain, Spillway,* and others. She's the author of several volumes of poetry and fiction, including the upcoming *Fourth Planet From the Sun* (© 2019 Rum Razor Press), and *Gondal Heights: A Bronte Tribute Anthology* (© 2019 Sybaritic Press) .

Rick Leddy is a cartoonist, poet and author. His poems have appeared in the Spectrum, Intersections and Altadena Poetry Review poetry anthologies. He has published two poetry collections: Metro Mona Lisa and 365+1: A Year of Beauty and Madness.

In 2019 **John B. Lee** was named recipient of the Norfolk County Heritage & Culture Dogwood Lifetime Achievement Award. The author of over seventy five books, his most recent publications are *Into a Land of Strangers* (Mosaic Press, 2019) and *Moths That Drink the Tears of Sleeping Birds* (Black Moss Press, 2019). He lives in a lake house overlooking Long Point Bay on the south coast of Lake Erie where he works as a full time author.

Linda Lerner's most recent publications include, *A Dance Around the Cauldron,* a prose work which takes place during the Salem witch trials, updated to present times, (LUMMOX Press, 2017); *The Ducks Were Real,* (NYQ Books, 2015) both nominated for a Pushcart Prize. Recent publications / acceptances include *Café Review, Trailer Park Quarterly, Wilderness Literary House Review, Cape Rock, Illumination Magazine & Piker Press. Taking the F Train,* forthcoming from NYQ books.

Bernice Lever, a poet and performer, creates poetry on Bowen Island. Her 10th book was *Small Acts,* (Black Moss Press, 2016). She edited *WAVES, Fine Canadian Literature,* at (York U.,

Toronto, 1972-1987). She is a Life Member of LCP, CAA & TOPS.. Bernice's travels have let her read poems on 5 continents. Her English text (now a free PDF) is *The Colour of Words*. Although she is active in many Canadian writing organizations, she is now on the west coast again, writing PEACE poems for World Poetry, etc. *www.colourofwords.com/wordpress*

Jane Lipman's first full-length poetry collection, *On the Back Porch of the Moon*, Black Swan Editions, 2012, won the 2013 New Mexico/Arizona Book Award and a 2013 NM Press Women's Award. Her chapbooks, *The Rapture of Tulips* and *White Crow's Secret Life*, Pudding House Publications, 2009, were finalists for NM Book Awards in Poetry in 2009 and 2010, respectively. Her poem "Unsung" won Second Prize in a national poetry contest, Honoring Cole Porter, 2015. She was First Runner Up in the LUMMOX Poetry Contest, 2016.

Ellaraine Lockie is widely published and awarded as a poet, nonfiction book author and essayist. *Tripping with the Top Down* is her thirteenth chapbook. Earlier collections have won Poetry Forum's Chapbook Contest Prize, San Gabriel Valley Poetry Festival Chapbook Competition, Encircle Publications Chapbook Contest, Best Individual Poetry Collection Award from *Purple Patch* magazine in England, and *the Aurorean's* Chapbook Choice Award. Ellaraine teaches writing workshops and serves as Poetry Editor for the lifestyles magazine, *Lilipoh*.

Radomir Vojtech Luza was born in Vienna, Austria in 1963 to renowned Czech parents. The SAG/AFTRA/AEA union actor is The Poet Laureate of North Hollywood, CA, a Pushcart Prize Nominee and the author of 30 books (26 collections of poetry) of which the latest poetry collection, *Sidewalks And Street Corners*, was published by Christian Faith Publishing in 2018. The veteran stand-up comedian has been penning poems for 33 years. He has had nearly 100 poems published in literary journals, anthologies, websites, newspapers, magazines and other media. To Luza, poetry is the literary bridge to God.

John Macker's most recent books are *Atlas of Wolves* and *The Blues Drink Your Dreams Away Selected Poems, 1983-2018*, both published by Stubborn Mule Press. Other works include *Gorge Songs*, 12 poems in 8 folios, a collaboration with woodblock artist Leon Loughridge, (Denver: DCArtPress, 2017/2018.) and *Disassembled Badlands*. Macker lives in Santa Fe, NM. He was also contributing editor to Albuquerque's Malpais Review. He won Mad Blood magazine's inaugural literary award for his long poem, "Wyoming Arcane."

Michael Mahoney was born in Wallingford with a mushroom-shaped left hip, Mahoney kills time giving birth to Imagination on the cave walls on his notebooks while he waits for the rest of the world to wake up, sipping cups of Infinity Tea and singing the dreams of our collective Ancestors. He's a firm believer in the written word over the meme, the typewritten over the digital. He agrees with the poet Huffstickler that the real revolution will be about feelings & perceptions, not about governments & killing people.

Georgia Santa Maria is a Native New Mexican, and is an artist, photographer and writer. Her books LichenKisses(2013), Dowsing (LUMMOX Press, 2017) and Berlin Poems and Photographs, co-written with Merimee Moffitt are available. She was the recipient of the LUMMOX Poetry Prize in 2016, and a First Place winner in 2018 with New Mexico Press Women for "Photography with Related Text," for Berlin Poems and Photographs, and an Honorable mention for the same from The National Federation of Press Women. Her most recent book, The My Ami Hippie Mommy Cookbook: how to be a kitchen diva without running water, a memoir of stories, photos, poems and recipes, came out in April of this year.

Mary McGinnis has been writing and living in New Mexico since 1972 where life has connected her with emptiness, desert, and mountains. Published in over 70 magazines and anthologies, she has also been nominated for a Pushcart Prize. She has published three full length collections: *Listening for Cactus* (1996), *October Again* (2008), *See with Your Whole Body* (2016). Her submission to a LUMMOX poetry contest (2017) won first prize, and publication of *Breath of Willow*. Mary frequently takes part in poetry readings in Santa Fe and Albuquerque, New Mexico and is available upon request for readings and poetry workshops.

Michael Meloan is a first place science fair winner at Henry Clay Jr. High. He lives in mid-Wilshire LA.

Basia Miller's poems have appeared in *Trickster, LUMMOX, Malpais Review,* and *the Santa Fe Literary Review* as well as in the French poetry journals *Poésie-sur-Seine* and *Portulan bleu.* Her bilingual chapbook, *The Next Village/Le prochain village,* translated by poet friends in France, was self-published in 2016. She has a second chapbook, *Backyard Tree/L'Arbre côté cour* (Paris : D'Ici et D'Ailleurs, Collection « Les Intuitistes, » 2017). Her translations of Francine Caron's poetry of place were republished in *Bibliophilie juBilatoire et Bilingue* in 2017. She is currently interested in French poet-songwriter and editor Pierre Seghers. She lives in Santa Fe.

Joseph Milosch graduated from San Diego State University. His poetry has appeared in various magazines, including the California Quarterly. He has multiple nominations for the Pushcart and received the Hackney Award for Literature. His books: *The Lost Pilgrimage Poems* and *Landscape of a Hummingbird,* were published by Poetic Matrix Press.

Elaine Mintzer is a Los Angeles poet who has been published in journals and anthologies including *Panoplyzine, Slipsteam, *82, Perspectives, Borders and Boundaries, Mom Egg Review, Subprimal Poetry Art, LUMMOX,* Lucid Moose Lit's *Like a Girl* anthology, *The Ekphrastic Review, Cultural Weekly, Rattle,* and *The Lindenwood Review* and *13 Los Angeles Poets.* Elaine's first collection, *Natural Selections,* was published by Bombshelter Press.

Michael Mirrola's publications include three Bressani Prize winners: the novel *Berlin* (2010); the poetry collection *The House on 14th Avenue* (2014); and the short story collection, *Lessons in Relationship Dyads* (2016). The short story, "A Theory of Discontinuous Existence," was selected for *The Journey Prize Anthology*; and "The Sand Flea" was a Pushcart Prize nominee. Born in Italy, raised in Montreal, Michael lives in Hamilton, Ontario. For more, visit his website: *www.michaelmirolla.com/index.html*

Tony Moffeit lives, writes, and sings the blues in Pueblo, Colorado. Along with Todd Moore, he co-founded the Outlaw Poetry Movement. His 2011 publication, *Born To Be Blue,* LUMMOX Press, was a finalist for the 2012 Colorado Book Award.

Marion Mutala has a master's degree in educational administration and taught for 30 years. She is the author of the bestselling and award-winning children's books, *Baba's Babushka: A Magical Ukrainian Christmas, Baba's Babushka: A Magical Ukrainian Easter, Baba's Babushka: A Magical Ukrainian Wedding and Kohkum's Babushka: A Magical Metis/ Ukrainian Tale.* She is also the author of *Grateful, The Time for Peace is Now, Ukrainian Daughter's Dance* (a poetry collection), *The Mechanic's Wife, More Baba's Please!* and *My Buddy, Dido! My Dearest Dido-* a book about the Ukrainian genocide- the Holodomor is her 11th book. Visit her website at: *www. babasbabushka.ca*

Evan Myquest, 70, lives in Sacramento with Eva, his wife of 43 years. Raised in North

Central Illinois, he packed in a life as a science fiction writer despite the fun of workshopping with Harlan Ellison, George RR Martin, and Gene Wolfe, and turned to poetry. His poetry can be found alongside Ferlinghetti, Hirschman, Patti Smith, Leonard Cohen and other poets across the U.S. Track him at *mmw50.com.*

Linda Neal studied literature at Pomona College. She later earned degrees in linguistics and clinical psychology, to become a licensed therapist. Her award-winning poems have appeared in numerous journals, including Beecher's, LUMMOX, Prairie Schooner Santa Fe Literary Journal, SLAB, Tampa Review. Her first collection, Dodge & Burn, came out in 2014. Third place winner in the Beyond Baroque foundation poetry competition in 2016, she's currently enrolled in an MFA poetry program at Pacific University. She lives near the beach with her dog, Mantra. She leads poetry workshops at the Redondo Beach Library, putters in her garden and likes making soup.

Ben Newel dropped out of the Bennington Writing Seminars during his first semester, eventually resuming his studies at Spalding University where he earned an MFA. His poems were nominated for *Best of the Net 2017.*

Terri Niccum's chapbook, *Looking Snow in the Eye,* was released in 2015 by Finishing Line Press. Recently, her poems have appeared in *Dark Ink: A Poetry Anthology Inspired by Horror,* and in *Cadence Collective* and the *Incandescent Mind anthologies, Volume 2* and *Selfish Work.* Her work has also been featured in *The Poeming Pigeon anthologies, From the Garden and Love Poems; Nimrod International Journal; The Maine Review; Oberon Poetry 2018; Literary Orphans; Angel City Review;* and *Pretty Owl Poetry.*

normal is no tourist, no phony poetaster, Ginsberg riffer, Whitmamesque street boy, but an authentic voice of the street, the real street,

singing a song as it was meant to be sung, in a time when such singing was possible...normal is the voice of the homeless, the victimized, the disaffected and the disturbed. These are poems born of the street, of the vagabond heart, the true restless American spirit that Whitman spoke of when he heard America singing. He has 2 chapbooks: *Blood on the Floor* and *American Child*; and a full-length collection: *I See Hunger's Children* (All published by LUMMOX Press).

Edward Nudelman's poetry collections include *Out Of Time, Running* (Harbor Mountain Press, 2014); *What Looks Like An Elephant* (2011, LUMMOX Press), received a Second Place for Indie Lit Awards Book of the Year; and *Night Fires* (2009, Pudding House Press), semifinalist for the OSU Press Journal Award. Nudelman's poems have recently appeared in *Rattle, Cortland Review, Valparaiso Review, Chiron Review, Evergreen Review, Poets and Artists, Ampersand, Syntax, The Atlanta Review, Mipoesias, Plainsongs, Floating Bridge Press,* and T*he Penwood Review,* and others. Nudelman owns and operates a rare bookshop in Seattle, which he founded in 1980.

John Pappas is an award winning American actor. He is a playwright, poet, painter and short story writer. Originally from Oakland, California he has lived in Los Angeles since 1974. He currently and for the last 18 years lives in Long Beach with his wife Caren and their three dogs Delilah, Youngster and Carver. He is extremely pleased and proud to have a second poem published in LUMMOX Press. *https://en.wikipedia.org/wiki/John_Pappas*

Jeannine M. Pitas published a chapbook, *thank you for dreaming*, with LUMMOX Press in 2018. The two poems published in this issue of the LUMMOX journal are from her first full-length collection, *Things Seen and Unseen*, which has just been published by Oakville, Ontario based Mosaic Press. She lives in Iowa and teaches at the University of Dubuque.

Charles Plymell *www.washburn.edu/reference/cks/mapping/plymell/index.html* or *www.vlib.us/beats/#plymell*

D.A. (David) Pratt "continues to continue" in a completely conventional community in a country called Canada. His spirit wants to be elsewhere – perhaps Prague or Paris.

Corrine Ramirez is a PCC Student with a thirst for knowledge and a desire to inspire by pushing the boundaries of life. Writing poetry, children's literature and other literary works has been a secret passion since childhood. Born into a life of medical impossibilities, numerous traumas, and abuse writing provided strength and endurance to carry on. Mother of two boys which was deemed medically impossible due to the nature of the vast medical conditions sustained throughout life. Given a life expectancy of 18 armed with determination now 41 and fiercely fighting *"to reach the unreachable star"* and prove that *"true love conquers all."*

Thelma T. Reyna's books have collectively won 14 national literary awards. She has written 5 books: a short story collection, 2 poetry chapbooks, and 2 full-length poetry collections, including her latest release, *Reading Tea Leaves After Trump* (2018), which won 6 national book awards in 2018 and was also a "2018 Book of the Year." Her fiction, poetry, and nonfiction have appeared in literary journals, anthologies, textbooks, blogs, and regional media for over 25 years. As Poet Laureate in Altadena, 2014-2016, she edited the *Altadena Poetry Review Anthology* in 2015 and 2016. She was a Pushcart Prize Nominee in Poetry in 2017.

Kevin Ridgeway is the author of *Too Young to Know* (Stubborn Mule Press). Recent work can be found in *Slipstream, Chiron Review, Nerve Cowboy, Big Hammer, Misfit Magazine, Trailer Park Quarterly, Main Street Rag* and *The American Journal of Poetry*, among others. He lives and writes in Long Beach, CA.

Judith Robinson* is an editor, teacher, fiction writer, poet and visual artist. A 1980 summa cum laude graduate of the University of Pittsburgh, she is listed in the **Directory of American Poets and Writers**. She has published 75+ poems, five poetry collections, one fiction collection; one novel; edited or co-edited eleven poetry collections. Teacher: Osher at Carnegie Mellon University and the University of Pittsburgh. Her newest collection, *Carousel*, was published in January, 2017, by LUMMOX Press.
*publication info & credits, art exhibitions, awards, including Pushcart nomination, on request.
www.judithrrobinson.com *alongtheserivers@gmail.com*

Dave Roskos is the editor of *Big Hammer* magazine and *Iniquity Press / Vendetta Books*. His books include *Fall & All* and *Lyrical Grain, Doggerel Chaff, & Pedestrian Preoccupations*. He lives in his home state of New Jersey with his wife the poet and collagist Jen Dunford-Roskos.

Jen Dunford-Roskos is from Providence RI. Her first poetry chapbook, *Shadow of Book*, with an introduction by the late Dave Church, was published by Iniquity Press/Vendetta Books in 2008. She lives in New Jersey with her husband, poet Dave Roskos, & several cats.

Dr. Gerard Sarnat won the Poetry in Arts First Place Award/Dorfman Prizes; has been nominated for Pushcarts plus Best of the Net Awards; authored *HOMELESS CHRONICLES* (2010), *Disputes* (2012), *17s* (2014) and *Melting The Ice King* (2016). He's widely published including recently by *New Ulster, Gargoyle, Stanford, Oberlin, Wesleyan, Johns Hopkins, Harvard, American Jewish University, Edinburgh, Columbia, Brown, Main Street Rag, American Journal Of Poetry, Poetry Quarterly, New Delta Review, Brooklyn Review, LA Review of Books, San Francisco Magazine, New York*

Times. MountAnalogue selected KADDISH for distribution nationwide Inauguration Day. Poetry was chosen for a 50th Harvard reunion Dylan symposium.

Patricia Scruggs lives and writes in Southern California. She is the author of *Forget the Moon* (2015). A retired high school art teacher, her work has appeared in *ONTHEBUS, Spillway, RATTLE, Calyx, Cultural Weekly, Crab Creek Review, LUMMOX* among others, as well as the anthologies *13 Los Angles Poets, So Luminous the Wildflowers,* and *Beyond the Lyric Moment.*

Michael C. Seeger lives with his lovely wife, Catherine, and still-precocious 16 year-old daughter, Jenetta, in a house owned by a magnificent Maine Coon (Jill) and two high-spirited Chihauhuas (Coco and Blue). He is an educator residing in the Coachella Valley near Palm Springs, California. Prior to his life as a middle school English instructor, Michael worked as a technical writer for a baseball card company and served as a Marine infantry officer during Desert Storm. Michael considers poetry a passion and writing a way of life. His poems have been published here and there in journals and such.

Lisa Segal, an L.A. artist/poet/writer, has two books—*Metamorphosis: Who is the Maker? An Artist's Statement* (her poetry, prose, and photographs of her sculptures) and the poetry/ prose collection *Trips* (with Josh Grapes and Olivia O. Wyatt). *Kicking Towards the Deep End* and *Method Writing: The Brush Up* are forthcoming (2019). She's the 2017 L.A. Poet Society Poetry Month Contest winner. She teaches poetry and writing through Los Angeles Poets & Writers. She's published in *Cultural Weekly, Serving House Journal, The Mas Tequila Review, KYSO, Dos Gatos Press, ONTHEBUS, The Thieving Magpie, Spectrum, Writing In A Woman's Voice, Poeticdiversity, FRE&D.* www.lisasegal.com

Nancy Shiffrin is the author of 3 collections of poetry: *The Vast Unknowing*, Infinity Publishing; *Game With Variations* and *Flight,* lulu.com. Her essays, reviews and articles are also collected on lulu.com, as is her script, *Allison's War.*

Doc Sigerson is a veteran of the army and makes his living in retail. His poetry has been published in *Unshod Quills, Hobo Camp Review, Unadorned Reader*, and his translations of Baudelaire and Neruda have appeared in *Unlikely Stories*. His poems, stories, essays, & reviews have appeared in Red Fez where he was an editor for a number of years.

Linda Singer is a local poet who hosts *Poetry Apocalypse* every third Sunday of the month at Angeles Gate Cultural Center in San Pedro. She can be reached through the Poetry Apocalypse website.

Judith Skillman's recent book is *Came Home to Winter*, Deerbrook Editions. She is the recipient of grants from Artist Trust & Academy of American Poets. Her poems have appeared in *Poetry, Cimarron Review, Zyzzyva, Nasty Women Poets, LUMMOX* & elsewhere. Visit *www.judithskillman.com*

Rick Smith wants you to check the website: *docricksmith.com* for his interview with Tom Waits, his new essay "Snowed In With Carl Sandburg," his harmonica wail on record and on soundtrack of Oscar nominated "Days of Heaven." Recent books: *Whispering In A Mad Dog's Ear; Hard Landing;* and *The Wren Notebook* (all LUMMOX Press). He is a Clinical Psychologist specializing in domestic violence and brain damage and practicing in Rancho Cucamonga, Calif.

Clifton Snider is the internationally celebrated author of eleven books of poetry, including *Moonman: New and Selected Poems* and *The Beatle Bump*, and four novels: *Loud Whisper,*

Bare Roots, Wrestling with Angels: A Tale of Two Brothers, and *The Plymouth Papers.* A political activist, he pioneered LGBTQ literary studies at California State University, Long Beach. A Jungian/Queer Literary critic, he has published hundreds of poems, short stories, reviews, and articles internationally, as well as the book, *The Stuff That Dreams Are Made On: A Jungian Interpretation of Literature.* He retired from teaching at California State University, Long Beach, in 2009.

Donna Snyder founded the Tumblewords Project in 1995 and continues to organize its free weekly workshop series and other events in the El Paso borderlands. Her poetry collections include *Poemas ante el Catafalco: Grief and Renewal* (Chimbarazu Press), *I Am South* (Virgogray Press), and *The Tongue Has its Secrets* (NeoPoiesis Press). Her poetry, fiction, and book reviews appear in such journals and anthologies as *Red Fez, Queen Mob's Teahouse, VEXT Magazine, Mezcla, Setu, Puerto del Sol, Inanna's Ascent*, and *Speak the Language of the Land.* She previously practiced law representing indigenous people, people with disabilities, and immigrant workers.

t. kilgore splake ("the cliffs dancer") lives in a tamarack location old mining row house in the ghost copper mining village of calumet in michigan's upper peninsula. splake has become a legend in the small press literary circles for his writing and photography. his most recent publication is *beyond brautigan creek.* this collection of poems also includes a dvd attachment. currently splake is working on a new poetry manuscript *the rosetta café ghosts* which will have a cover photograph resembling edward hopper's "nighthawks" painting.

MG Stephens exists.

Jeanine Stevens is the author of *Limberlost and Inheritor* (Future Cycle Press). Her first poetry collection, *Sailing on Milkweed* was published by Cherry Grove Collections. Winner of the MacGuffin Poet Hunt, The Stockton Arts Commission Award, The Ekphrasis Prize and WOMR Cape Cod Community Radio National Poetry Award. *Brief Immensity*, won the Finishing Line Press Open Chapbook Award. Jeanine recently received her sixth Pushcart Nomination. She participated in Literary Lectures sponsored by Poets and Writers. Work has appeared in *North Dakota Review, Pearl, Stoneboat, Rosebud, Chiron Review*, and *Forge.* Jeanine studied poetry at U.C. Davis and California State University, Sacramento.

Kevin Patrick Sullivan's books include, *First Sight, The Space Between Things, Under Such Brilliance* and *UNIMPAIRED.* His poems are in *SOLO, ASKEW, LUMMOX, MIRAMAR* and several other anthologies. He is co-editor of Corners of the Mouth A Celebration of Thirty Years at the Annual San Luis Obispo Poetry Festival. A Poet Laureate Emeritus for the city of San Luis Obispo and the Co-founder and Co-Curator of the Annual San Luis Obispo Poetry Festival and the monthly reading series Corners of the Mouth held at Linnaea's Café since 1984.

Patti Sullivan's chapbooks include *At The Booth Memorial Home For Unwed Mothers 1966; For The Day;* and *Not Fade Away.* Poems appear in *LUMMOX, Cloudbank, Solo Novo, Hummingbird, Raising Lilly Ledbetter-Women Poets Occupy the Workspace* and in *Miramar.* She is co-director of the Annual San Luis Obispo Poetry Festival and the monthly series Corners of the Mouth. She is a poetry editor with Evening Street Press. Her artwork has appeared on several journals and books as well as being exhibited in one woman shows and group shows.

Lynn Tait, an award-winning poet/photographer residing in Sarnia Ontario, has published poems in *Windsor Review,*

Contemporary Verse II, Freefall, Vallum, Literary Review of Canada, seven issues of *LUMMOX* and in over 100 anthologies. Her photos/digital art have appeared on the covers of seven poetry books. She is a member of the League of Canadian Poets and The Ontario Poetry Society and co-founder of the Sarnia poetry workshop After Hours Poets.

G. Murray Thomas recently moved to rural upstate New York from Long Beach, CA. Without the distractions of SoCal, he has plenty of time to ponder weird things. Someday he may put all those ponderings into a book.

H. Lamar Thomas continues living a secluded life with his rescue Daisy the old white Boxer; meditating, contemplating, reading post WWII poetry, writing endless notebooks of poetry and a piano piece a week. Waiting for the New America to die off and get back to the real America. Published over 700 works, most of which I have no idea where they are because my last dog literally ate many of the books. Repeated Apple updates destroyed my last back up drive along with poetry. Still putting it all together again. Georgia. Always back to Georgia.

Mary Langer Thompson's poems, short stories, and essays appear in various journals and anthologies. She is a contributor to two poetry writing texts, *The Working Poet* (Autumn Press, 2009) and *Women and Poetry: Writing, Revising, Publishing and Teaching* (McFarland, 2012), and was the 2012 Senior Poet Laureate of California. A retired school principal and former secondary English teacher, Langer Thompson received her Ed.D. from the University of California, Los Angeles. She continues to enjoy

conducting writing workshops for schools, prisons, and in her community of the high desert of California.

Bill Tremblay is a poet, novelist, reviewer. He has published nine full-length volumes including *Crying in the Cheap Seats* [University of Massachusetts Press], *The Anarchist Heart* [New Rivers Press]. *Home Front* [Lynx House Press]. *Second Sun: New & Selected Poems* [L'Eperiver Press]. *Duhamel: Ideas of Order in Little Canada* [BOA Editions Ltd.], *Rainstorm Over the Alphabet* [Lynx House Press], *Shooting Script: Door of Fire* [Eastern Washington University Press] which won the Colorado Book Award, as well as *Magician's Hat: Poems on the Life and Art of David Alfaro Siqueiros* [Lynx House Press] and most recently *Walks Along the Ditch: Poems*, Lynx House Press [2016].

Maja Trochimczyk, Ph.D., is a music historian, poet and photographer; author of seven books on music, five volumes of poetry, three anthologies, and hundreds of poems and research studies published in over 50 journals. She read papers at nearly 90 conferences and received awards from: the Polish Ministry of Culture, American Council of Learned Societies, Polish American Historical Association, McGill University, and others. She is the President of Moonrise Press and of Helena Modjeska Art and Culture Club, as well as Acting President of California State Poetry Society and Secretary and Communications Director of the Polish American Historical Association.

Wyatt Underwood hosts or co-hosts three sequences of open mics, in Encino-Tarzana, in

Westwood, and in Venice. He participates in open mics scattered around Los Angeles. You can find his work in local anthologies and on his Facebook page.

Rolland Vasin (aka Vachine) , a third generation American writer, published in the anthologies *Wide Awake, Coiled Serpent, LUMMOX, Spectrum,* and *Extreme,* among others, Features at local literary performance venues including Beyond Baroque, The World Stage, Expressions L.A. and reads open-mics from Cambridge MA to Big Sur CA. The Laugh Factory's 1992 3rd Funniest CPA in LA, his day job includes Single Audits of child, family, and research non-profits as well as Auxiliaries of the California State University system. A resident of Santa Monica, Vachine tries to play guitar, banjo, ukulele, and harmonica, but not all at the same time.

Richard Vidan has been fired from many low-paying manual-labor jobs. His poetry has previously been published in LUMMOX. His paintings have also been featured in LUMMOX and his painting "Red Sun Black Water" was the cover of LUMMOX 6. A poet and Outsider Artist for 40-plus years, his paintings are held in a number of private collections. As an actor with no formal training, he has appeared and performed in numerous TV shows, movies, and stage plays. He is a frondeur and an otherwise criminal restrained by the bounds of politeness. His personal motto: Live as if you are already dead.

Stewart Warren author of over 25 poetry collections, is a drifter and evocateur whose work is both personal and transpersonal with a mystic undercurrent. His heart-wise images evoke secret fire and suggest pathways perpendicular to the slave trade matrix of world society. Stewart is the owner of Mercury HeartLink, an independent New Mexico press that supports writers in realizing their artistic visions.

Linda Whittenberg's writing has a distinctly Midwestern flavor, at least she thinks so because it seems growing up in Illinois corn country influences--subject matter, voice, rhythm of the words. She has published five volumes of poetry. Of these, *Tender Harvest*, 2009, Black Swan Editions, was Finalist for the NM Book Award. Her work has been widely published in the U.S. and abroad. She has traveled to Ireland many times for literary conferences and because she considers it another home. Her book, *Somewhere in Ireland*, tells in poetry and prose the story of her connection with that country.

Pamela Williams is a poet, visual artist, and writer, with a fine art/design degree from Indiana University, and a lifelong habit of artistic expression. Her grounded upbringing in the heartland provided the springboard for thirty expansive years in the San Francisco area, where the vibrant culture, spectacular geography, and her antique business offered a parade of provocative fodder for her writing. New Mexico's extreme contrasts and rich history are now fueling alchemical inspiration through its proffered seductions and mysterious remnants of multi-cultural heritage, feeding her current poetry/assemblage work and her first collection of poetry, Hair on Fire, available at amazon.com: *http://amzn.to/2eD5lxL* .

Felice Zoota-Lucero considers herself to be a poet in disguise, product owner for software used by hospitals by day and poet by night. With multiple features in Los Angeles and a handful of published works, she aspires to connect with humans in meaningful ways while finding balance through love of her family, dogs, and yoga. "Smile, it gives your face something to do" was her high school yearbook quote. She was unknowingly onto something as life can have unexpected challenges, but applying a positive twist and a smile can make everything better. Find her at *FZLpoet.com*.

72948827R00122

Made in the USA
Columbia, SC
04 September 2019